RESTAURANT PROMOTION AND PUBLICITY

For Just A Few Dollars A Day

By Tiffany Lambert

The Food Service Professionals Guide To:
Restaurant Promotion And Publicity
For Just A Few Dollars A Day: 365 Secrets Revealed

Atlantic Publishing Group, Inc. Copyright © 2003
1210 SW 23rd Place
Ocala, Florida 34474
800-541-1336
352-622-5836 - Fax

www.atlantic-pub.com - Web Site
sales@atlantic-pub.com E-mail

SAN Number :268-1250

International Standard Book Number: 0-910627-14-2

Library of Congress Cataloging-in-Publication Data

Lambert, Tiffany.
Promoting & generating publicity for your restaurant for just
a few dollars a day : 365 secrets revealed / by Tiffany
Lambert.
p. cm. -- (The food service professionals guide to ; 4)
Includes bibliographical references and index.
ISBN 0-910627-14-2 (pbk. : alk. paper)
1. Restaurants--Public relations.   I. Title. II. Title:
Promoting and generating publicity for your restaurant for
just a few dollars a day. III. Series.
TX911.3.P77L36 2003
659.2'964795--dc21

2002010832

Printed in Canada

Book layout and design by Meg Buchner of Megadesign
www.mega-designs.com • e-mail: megadesn@mhtc.net

CONTENTS

Promotion and publicity are necessary for your restaurant's survival.

INTRODUCTION

Fact: You could open a restaurant with the perfect ambiance, the best-tasting food and the crème-de-la-crème of servers, but if you don't promote it properly, it will fail. Publicity and promotions are that important to the survival of any business, particularly in the food industry.

It's a world where presentation, appeal and service are of the utmost importance, yet many restaurateurs falsely believe those three elements are enough to generate the pull their establishments need in order to flourish.

Advertising is an expense in which many can't, or don't want to, invest. In a major city newspaper, a small, black-and-white ad the size of a standard business card costs anywhere from $100 to $1,000 for one weekday!

Is it any wonder why restaurants avoid pouring money into ad campaigns? It's a catch-22 situation: if you advertise, you're probably not going to recoup the investment, but if you don't, you'll lose just as much, if not more, money in the end from lack of exposure.

Restaurant Promotion & Publicity For Just A Few Dollars A Day: 365 Secrets Revealed shows you how to promote your business without spending a fortune! The ideas and practical tips contained in this guide are just what you need to help boost your sales and your standing in the community. Make your marketing efforts more than pay for themselves.

Every single one of these suggestions can be implemented in just one day. What's more, all of them are wallet-friendly concepts that any restaurant can use. From promotional concepts to leveraging the power of the press to boosting your sales, this guide has it all!

To begin, the following pages will teach you how to get FREE press. The kind where you don't pay a dime! What can free press do for you? Let's take two examples:

- You open the "Food" section of your daily paper and see a small, black-and-white ad for a Mexican-food restaurant. It has the logo, a catchy phrase about how they're "the best," the hours they're open and a number to call if you need directions.

- In the same paper, the food columnist has written a story about another Mexican-food restaurant on the same side of town - one that's holding a special fiesta where every meal sold raises a certain amount of money for charity. Oh, and by the way, the food is to die for, notes the columnist.

Where are you going for dinner that night? There's no question which ad is more powerful: the one that didn't pay for its coverage!

CHAPTER ONE

THE POWER OF THE PRESS

Holiday Headlines to Heighten Your Success

Holidays are considered to be one of the most effective natural marketing tools in our society. Many grocery stores begin selling Christmas items in August. Valentines hit the shelves December 26 and Halloween creeps around in mid-July.

Use the holidays to promote your restaurant in the media, not just in-house. All you have to do is send a press release to the local papers and radio stations so that the editor can use your story as a feature item.

For all examples in this publication, the fictitious restaurant name Rose's is used for illustration purposes. Here are 12 headlines and ideas (one for each month) you can use to promote your restaurant to the press.

- **January.** "Rose's Restaurant Brings Good Luck to Patrons with Free Black-Eyed Pea Party New Year's Day from 11 a.m.-9 p.m." Black-eyed peas are free with every meal. It's a Southern tradition, but many regions have their own New Year's Day superstitions.

- **February.** "One Lucky Couple Who Gets Engaged at Rose's Restaurant on Valentine's Day

Will Win a Complete Wedding and Honeymoon Package." Sounds pricey, doesn't it? Not if you let others pay for it all! You can easily find companies willing to donate their services (a free wedding cake, for example) in exchange for the coverage they'll get in the promotion - all you have to do is ask.

- **March.** "The Easter Bunny Hops Over to Rose's Restaurant for Week of Free Pictures and Egg-Coloring Contest." Rent a bunny costume and hand out Polaroid pictures to patrons who want to meet The Bunny himself. Once at the table, they can color in a preprinted Easter picture for a chance to win $25 in Rose Bucks (play money that will bring the party back in for a second visit). For those who don't win, give a coupon as a "runners-up" prize.

- **April.** "April Is National Zoo and Aquarium Month - Eat at Rose's Restaurant to Receive One Free Ticket to the Dallas Zoo or Aquarium." Partner with the zoo to give the coupons away. You don't lose a cent, and the zoo gets press coverage and patronage.

- **May.** "Rose's Restaurant Is Donating 10% of Every Purchase in May to the Warren Nursing Home in Honor of Senior Citizens' Month."

- **June.** "On June 27, National Decide to Be Married Day, Rose's Restaurant Will Give One Lucky Couple a One-Carat Diamond Engagement Ring from Smith's Jewelers." Two establishments split the cost on one ring, and both get free press and extra business.

- **July.** "Uncle Sam and President Bush to Visit with Diners July 4 at Rose's Restaurant." Almost every major city has look-alikes for hire for special occasions. If not, rent a costume and hand it over to one of your waitstaff. You can get free press and give your customers a night of excitement – when they enjoy meeting two famous historical figures in one night!

- **August.** "Mad at Your Spouse? On August 25, National Kiss and Make-Up Day, Rose's Restaurant Is Holding a Lip-Locking Contest Where One Lucky Couple Will Receive a Night of Romance at the Hathaway Hotel, Followed by a Carriage Ride through Downtown Dallas."

- **September.** "Bring Your Kids to Rose's Back-to-School Special Where Kids Eat Free the First Week of Classes." Here's an added tidbit: September 26 is National Food Service Employees Day; while this may not be newsworthy information, do some in-house promotion to boost the staff's tip income for the day.

- **October.** "Rose's Restaurant Hosts Halloween Costume Party - Best in Show Wins $100 Prize." In the next several sentences, tell them that Polaroid photos of the costumes will be taken throughout the night. One winner will be selected to receive $100 cash. The entry form, complete with name, address and phone number, is a great way to capture mailing information for future mailers.

- **November.** "Rose's Restaurant to Donate 10 Turkeys to Homeless for Every 100 Customers Who Eat at Rose's During the Month of November."

- **December.** "Santa to Host Tree-Decorating Festivities at Rose's Restaurant - Bring a Wrapped Toy for Needy Children and Get Your Picture Taken Free." A Polaroid, a Santa costume and your standard Christmas tree each patron gets to decorate with an ornament gets you recognized as a fun establishment that cares about the needs of the community.

Seven Secrets to Marketing to the Mind-Set of the Media

When we think of the media, we think of the Big Three: television, radio and print. Use all of them to get free or inexpensive attention for your restaurant, just by following the standard rules and regulations that media officials expect when your paperwork comes across their desks. Use these "Seven Secrets" to play up your position in the press and win unbiased, unpaid-for endorsement from those powerful sources of information we all look to for guidance and facts on the best and worst of what life has to offer.

- **Give your press release a newsworthy appeal.** Remember, this is not an ad, so your content must be written as news - and have a newsworthy approach. No bragging that you're "the best." Leave out the boastful text, or your press release will wind up in the trash. Need a professional to write one for you? Go to

www.WriteConsultants.com or www.elance.com:
they'll deliver a document that will garner you
the coverage that you seek.

- **Try to connect your headline to current
  events.** As you learned in the last section, using
  holidays is a great incentive for editors to give
  you free coverage. It doesn't have to be a
  holiday, though: if the economy is hit hard,
  come up with a slogan and idea related to that!

- **Give it a local angle.** You're more likely to get
  coverage from your local stations or publications
  than you are from international or national
  outlets. And who are your customers, anyway?
  The locals and people visiting the area!

- **Answer the "Five Ws."** In the first paragraph,
  preferably the very first sentence, tell the
  audience Who, What, When, Where and Why (or
  how).

- **Stick to standard submission rules.** Use plain
  white 8-1/2" x 11" paper, sent in by whatever
  method each outlet says it wants. Some will
  prefer mail, others fax, but avoid e-mailing it as
  an attachment - especially if it's unsolicited!

- **Give them more than one way to get in touch
  with you.** The editor probably won't print your
  press release as is, but will get a staff member to
  contact you for more information so he or she can
  write a story. Don't rely on one cell phone
  number: give them e-mail and mailing addresses
  and more than one number where they can reach
  you.

- **Don't call us, we'll call you.** Yes, it's hard to sit back and wonder whether or not you'll get your story printed. And if not, you want to know why! But it's best to avoid calling the editor and interrupting his or her workday for questions like this - you might risk being labeled a pest and not get any coverage in the future! Need more press release tips? Visit www.infoscavenger.com/prtips.htm for some no-nonsense help in this area.

Cashing In on Community Contributions

You don't have to feel guilty about wanting your community involvement to reflect nicely on your business and pull in more profits. Most companies have entire departments dedicated to handling their charity interactions, and they all do it wisely - to the benefit of the company and society. Here are eight promotions you can implement to show your support for the society and cash in on the coverage you get as a result:

- **Hold an on-site blood drive.** Call your local blood bank and see if they'll bring out one of their portable vehicles to set up in your parking lot. You might also want to offer a coupon or free dessert to any customer or visitor who donates blood. Contact www.redcross.org/donate to find out how to start a program.

- **Raise money for a children's hospital.** One way to get people to donate a lot of money is to have a 12-by-12 drive. That means they agree to donate $12 per month (an easy amount for most people to handle) for 12 months! That's $144 per person! Imagine if only 100 people agree to it - that's $14,400 you've raised!

- **Sponsor a children's sports team.** Most cities have an underprivileged kids' sports center. Send a press release to announce that every purchase means a 10 percent donation to the foundation for kids.

- **Build a home for the needy.** Habitat for Humanity is a great organization that, in a very short time, actually puts a roof over a needy family's heads. Put your staff to work on a voluntary basis and build ten homes in one month for added effect!

- **Have a book drive.** Every customer who brings in a new children's book gets one free dessert. Donate the collection to a local library.

- **Raise funds for awareness.** Breast cancer, Down's Syndrome, AIDS, etc. Look up various awareness holidays and promote the fact that a portion of your proceeds will go to research on these diseases.

- **Raise funds for prevention.** Spousal abuse, substance abuse, teen violence, etc. Raise money for education to prevent certain headline-grabbing society dilemmas. Contact the National Coalition Against Domestic Violence to learn more.

- **Raise funds for safety.** Fire safety, gun safety, child-care safety, etc. You can bring in professional firefighters, police officers or CPR experts to meet with your clientele and hand out their own stickers, pamphlets and other items for the classes that they offer.

Prize Packages Worthy of the Press

When you offer a prize, that's good enough to garner the attention of the press, your only cost will be for the prize itself, and not the associated coverage. If I had the kind of money it takes to pay out a big prize, I might as well pay for a big ad, you say. Not necessarily! First of all, an advertisement won't bring in nearly as many customers - customers you can count on to return, provided the service and fare are up to their standards. Secondly, it doesn't cost a lot of money to offer a prize if you do it one of two ways. Consider the following:

- **Get covered.** Many insurance companies will offer specific prize payout coverage if you offer a contest where someone might win eventually. Think of the burger contests where you save up three or more matching tickets. Rarely do the winners pay attention and save up matching tickets. The one they need is very hard to come by. So go ahead - offer that $1 million prize! Companies like IC Group Inc., www.icgroupinc.com/MainSite/Main.htm, specialize in prize management, including insurance coverage!

- **Team up with the manufacturer of the prize.**
  Many companies will give away their products
  just for the coverage they'll get during your
  promotion. If you combine your promotion with
  a charity, you'll get even better prizes and more
  coverage! Whenever you do a prize promotion,
  don't just cater to the local print publications,
  approach other dealers who might want a piece
  of the action as well. Be sure to let your other
  media contacts in on the promotion, because
  many will want to send out a crew to cover it if
  the crowd and the prize are big enough!
  Remember that it doesn't hurt to just ask manufacturers or dealers. If you're shy, at least send a
  letter to the highest position you're able to get a
  name for and see what he or she has to say. Try
  the following novel approach:

- **Contact boat dealers/manufacturers** to see if
  they'd be willing to donate a wave runner for a
  big promotion you're having. Let them set up an
  area at your restaurant where they can give
  away brochures and talk to customers one-on-
  one if they wish.

- **If you're offering a wave runner by one manufacturer**, why not call up a water accessory
  retailer to see if they want to give away life
  preservers with it, or scuba gear - a whole sea-
  faring package!

Whom you talk to is just as important as what you intend to say in your message. If you want the publicity that your establishment deserves, you have to seek out the most influential prospects and then make them believe in you. Here are five tips to help you get the press on your side and maximize the possibilities of media coverage throughout the year:

- **First, understand whom it is you're seeking.** Media contacts are from every race, religion, gender and region you can imagine. The worlds of television, radio and print are vastly different, and all will have their own individual standards and requirements. You can find out whom the government uses at www.gcs.gov.mo to learn more.

- **Start making a list and checking it twice.** Developing a media contact list will be the backbone of your publicity strategy. Once you're "in" with the right people, they'll come to you for updates, instead of you having to ask them every so often. When you're coming up with a list of viable names, be sure to double-check the spelling and ensure that the name is current. You don't want to send a press release to an editor that hasn't worked there in two years.

- **In the restaurant business, it never hurts to give the press a free pass to experience your food for themselves.** Invite them for a free meal, courtesy of the house, and have them ask for you so that you get to meet and greet (and form a relationship with) them personally. A little bit of kindness goes a long way.

- **If they won't come to you, then you go to them.** That's right. If they turn down the invitation or never show up, send a staff member to the publication or station to deliver free desserts to the editor - and maybe even his staff! Sugarcoating the situation never hurts.

- **Offer exclusive information to only one source.** Pick one media source - preferably the one most likely to give you coverage - and send them a press release. State specifically that the information you're sharing isn't being made available to anyone other than them. It'll go a long way to grease the wheels. Once the story breaks, you'll probably be approached by other media contacts that saw the story and also want the specifics. At that time, it's okay to share the original press release.

Two Ways to Make Sure the Media Bias Is on Your Side

We're trained to believe that all the media are unbiased in what they report to the public. Wrong! In the food industry in particular, everything the media reports has to do with opinions. If the food editor of your newspaper doesn't care for Tex-Mex, and that's what you serve, don't count on him or her ever reviewing your establishment. If he or she does, prepare yourself for a less-than-kind review. There are a couple of ways around it, however! Consider the following:

- **Do some research.** Go to the library and do a quick review of the articles in the archive of his or her past articles over the last year. Find out what some of the reviewer's idiosyncrasies were - and make sure your staff pay close attention to detail whenever this journalist comes in for a visit.

- **Advertise a little bit.** You can count on the editor checking to see if you're a customer with them, before he or she encourages others to become customers of yours. At least once or twice, commit to a small advertisement. Keep in mind that the paper doesn't make money on the $0.50-per-copy retail sale, but rather the ad rates that they charge businesses like yourself!

- **Bias.** Like it or not, media contacts are human too. Although they normally stick to reporting with a level of fairness few others can achieve, they can't help but interject a bit of bias. In fact, most publications are known for being politically liberal or conservative. Coverage of the food industry is not exempt from personal opinion. When doing a promotion, keep this in mind, as you will be partnering with other groups that the press may or may not want to cover.

Season Finale Showcase

If you really want the local news station to cover your restaurant in-house, then be sure to start a major promotion around the time the season finales hit the screens. Here are five ways you can cater to the corps of press who will love your ideas:

- **Become the official viewing headquarters.** All it takes is a blanket statement declaring yourself the official viewing headquarters, and you become just that! Which station is going to tell you not to promote its show?

- **Dress up your restaurant.** The hit TV show "Survivor" always has a specific theme - "Africa," "Island" - you name it. Decorate in the same theme and make the patrons feel as if they're "in the show" for a night. Find out how to decorate and everything you need to know at www.cbs.com/primetime/survivor4.

- **Hold a look-alike contest.** Is he as hairy as Bunky from Big Brother? Does he look like a current or past president? Or does she look like a famous movie star? Let patrons participate in a look-alike contest where the winner walks away with a prize.

- **Bring in a big-screen TV.** It just won't do to have a small screen mounted on top of the bar. Borrow or rent a big-screen TV for the event so that everyone will gather around in the bar area and put on a good, enthusiastic show for the media.

- **Picker prizes.** Hold a contest for whoever is able to pick the winner of the show's season finale. Dinner on the house or a discount meal should entice viewers to come in for the night.

Inviting the Press to Be a Part of Your Publicity

Employees of TV stations, radio stations and print publications love to be a part of the fun. Don't just tell them about it - invite them to take part in the event as your special guests! It's much more compelling for the audience to hear and see coverage taking place at the scene than it is to hear a blurb about the event. Here are some suggestions to help you attract publicity:

- **Old-fashioned dunking booths.** If you hold a small carnival in your parking lot or at a local park, you can have a cakewalk, face painting and dunking booth that gives customers a chance to have fun and meet a local celebrity at the same time. Don't know where to rent one? Build your own. Everything you need to know is at www.handymanusa.com.

- **See if the fun and wacky radio DJ wants to be the dunking victim.** The station will love blasting their tunes at the event and handing out prizes and T-shirts while they're at it!

- **Give them emcee responsibilities.** You can combine charitable community contributions with publicity and press schmoozing just by letting them have the spotlight.

- **Contact your local A Wish with Wings.** This charity fulfills terminally ill children's wishes and offers to make one of their dreams come true. Hold a fund-raiser beforehand to cover the costs. Then call up the media to host the event - on you! For instance, one child in Texas wanted to experience snow, for real. Since it doesn't snow much in Texas, a radio station hired a professional snow-machine operator to fill the child's yard with the white powdery ice before she woke up one morning. The station's top DJ reported live from the scene, melting everyone's hearts – but not the snow!

In-House Promos

Don't forget to pay close attention to the way you promote your business to people who are already in the house. It's just as important to factor in-house customers into your publicity campaign as it is to drive in new customers. The purpose of in-house promotions is to impress these customers into coming back a second time. If they see others are oohing and aahing over your establishment, they'll automatically have a good impression to begin with. Here are some things you can do to boost first impressions when customers walk in the door:

- **Frame 'em and hang 'em.** Any time the local paper writes an article or review about your restaurant, cut it out and frame it. Then start building a wall of praise somewhere in the lobby, where customers will see it the moment they walk in the door.

- **Use quotes in your materials.** Has a customer given a great testimonial, or has a newsperson raved about your place of business? If so, ask permission to use the quote in your promotional materials.

- **Document events with pictures.** At all of your promotional events, get a camera and start documenting the fun! Many restaurants have framed pictures of their events hanging on the walls of the lobby and around the restaurant.

Professionalizing Your Publicity with Striking Logos

When approaching the press in the hope of getting free publicity and coverage for your events, you want to ensure your restaurant has an effective, professional logo to go along with it. Here are five ways to increase your coverage by using a brand image that conveys the style and atmosphere of your establishment:

- **Have it professionally designed.** You can get a professional logo for as little as $199. The investment is well worth the return. Set your logo apart from the usual ones in the restaurant business; sometimes the abstract is more memorable. You can order a logo online at www.1800mylogo.com, or choose a professional freelance designer, such as www.mega-designs.com.

- **Slather your name all over the place.** You can't use a logo too much. On napkins, signs, bags, cards, matches, receipts and menus - leave no space unfilled. Your logo will be ingrained in their memories long after they leave. At www.gopromos.com, if you enter the promotional code YH901, you'll get a 15 percent discount off your first online order!

- **Sell T-shirts.** In the original *Cheers* bar in Boston, Massachusetts, you'll find an entire wall of special T-shirts emblazoned with the *Cheers* logo. You can go the same way; follow in the footsteps of the Hard Rock Café and Joe's Crab Shack - every time a customer wears it, you'll be getting free publicity. The most important part of this chemistry is an enticing logo. Try www.restonshirt.com to have yours professionally designed.

- **Plant it on take-away cups.** Many restaurants offer kids cups' of reusable plastic, but grown-ups appreciate it, too! Your logo will be facing them every time they open their cupboards to quench their thirst. Find a great deal at www.raggo.com.

- **Serve the fare on a Frisbee.** During summer months, turn a Frisbee emblazoned with your logo on the top, upside-down, and serve the meal in it. At www.branders.com, you can find the perfect disc for your needs!

Understand the difference between promotion and publicity.

CHAPTER TWO

PROMOTIONAL BASICS YOUR BUSINESS CAN'T LIVE WITHOUT

Promotional Staples

In the food service business, there are certain staples, just like the ones that stock your shelves, which must be used as part of the publicity and promotional dishes you serve to the public. Bear in mind the following:

- **Promotions are different from publicity.** Understand the difference.

  - Publicity is media coverage.
  - A promotion, on the other hand, uses the gimmicks and tricks of the trade that make people want to visit your establishment.

- **Promotional tactics.** Study the competition. Adapt and disguise their ideas.

- **Promotions should be offered on a regular basis.** Everyone, even customers, think in terms of "What have you done for me lately?" With that in mind, you have to remember that just one promotion won't do it. Two won't, either. To keep your business in the front of the ever-watchful eye of the public, you have to promote as often as possible - each time getting bigger and better than before!

First, let's define what "cocktail hour" really means. Contrary to what some people believe, cocktail hour is not a musical, high-energy time to rev up your customers - or put them to sleep! Cocktail hour is a time when coworkers come in to unwind and talk about all of the good, bad and ugly that happened at work that day. It's also a deal-striking hour. Many corporate executives arrange to meet their clients at cocktail hour to finalize some of the best and biggest deals in existence! So how do you cater to the cocktail-hour camaraderie phenomenon? Like this:

- **Offer drink specials to loosen up the atmosphere.** Half-priced drinks, decorative umbrella drinks and extra-large drinks will lift the mood and bring smiles to the faces of your customers.

- **Avoid overserving.** Make sure your bartender and waitstaff keep an eye on cocktail hour customers. Don't run the risk of overserving someone and becoming liable for his or her actions later. Most people want only one or two drinks and some snacks while they wait, so it's not a major concern.

- **Give away snacks.** Whether it's a bowl full of peanuts or pistachios or a buffet of small appetizer specials, customers will appreciate your cocktail concoction and will stick around for their full meal later that evening!

- **Offer relaxation.** Cocktail hour is not the time for a live band or blaring music. People are there to unwind, and you'll be wasting your money if the entertainment is so loud that they can't hear over it. Make the lighting lower than normal and the ambiance friendly. That's all you need to do to create a winning cocktail affair.

• **Remember that cocktail hour is not the time to make a lot of money.** It will make you money in the long run, but not at that exact moment. How will it make money for you? People are loyal to their cocktail-hour establishments. Your clients will become regulars, and your restaurant bar will be the one place they'll be able to come to feel extra special.

• **Boost your waitstaff's memory.** You want them to cultivate friendly relationships with your customers (provided the customer feels like reciprocating the pleasantries). The more names they remember, the more clients who'll feel like "one of the gang" and will want to return daily or weekly to spend money with you!

Meeting Their Question with an Answer

If you've ever worked in an office building, you've heard the question, "Where do we eat today?" It's probably the most common question in offices everywhere. It becomes a ritual for the staff to order together from one place, whether or not the boss is splurging for it. Here are some ways to give them an answer to their question so that you profit and they don't have to think about it anymore. Try the following tactics:

- **Let people know about you.** You can go to business parking lots nearby and place flyers on the employees' windshields. Get your copies made at www.kinkos.com, and they'll bring the shipment to you!

- **Go to where the buck stops.** You can put together a special promo package for business owners and managers so they'll know you offer a place to bring a group whenever a coworker retires or is promoted.

- **Sample them silly!** If there's a really big office somewhere in the nearby vicinity, have one of your staff deliver a one-time sampling of your entrees, appetizers or desserts. You don't have to deliver enough for everyone - just enough for some of the people to taste it and brag about how delicious it was!

- **Advertise with every order.** Someone ordered for the first time for delivery at a new building? Be sure to send them some coupons for their next delivery order! Just like the ones stuck on every pizza delivery box, your coupons should have your name and number, making it easy to order again. Expiration dates will ensure that the coupons are cashed in sooner rather than later.

- **Why you?** Answering this question is the easy part: because you're offering them... something tasty...a free sample to tempt them...a cocktail hour promotion...a fun or relaxing atmosphere. Whatever your best attributes are, tout them as much as you can!

Building Your Business with Balloons

Balloons. They're festive. They're cheap. They can bring you a lot of extra business! There's something about having balloons around that lightens everyone's mood and makes kids smile. Children especially love balloons of every shape, size and color. It doesn't have to be anything fancy – just filled is good enough for them! If you're going to go with a balloon campaign, learn the best ways to do it:

- **Use helium if at all possible.** You can rent a helium machine for next to nothing, and the difference between those and the ones you make your staff blow up will be BIG in the eyes of the customer!

- **Fill them with extras, too!** The great thing about balloons is that they're not limited to gases for fillers. You can make water balloons or you can fill them with prizes! Put coupons or small plastic toys inside and let each customer "win" something when you give away these balloons.

- **Put your name on them.** Purchase large quantities of balloons personalized with your establishment's name on them, for a relatively small fee. Or, buy the balloons, blow them up, and stamp them with your own business stamp before any big event. Have them personalized at www.victorystore.com. You can get 25,000 balloons for only $115!

- **Think strategic placement.** Give them away at the door; put them at, or bring them to, the table; or bunch them up all around the place for an added effect of fun! Even consider putting them on the roof, if it's legal in your area.

Driving 'Em Back Again and Again

Gaining new customers is the easy part. Getting them to come back time after time is where the real strategy comes about. It's not enough to have your service sparkle and your servers shine. Today's customers have a plethora of options at their disposal, and they have to have a pretty good reason to choose you above all others. So how can you ensure success and beat out the other guys all at the same time? Consider the following possibilities:

- **Use the old haircut tactic.** Many barbershops offer customer frequency cards that customers can have "punched" every time they come in for a visit. You can do the same with your restaurant promotion. For instance, after the second visit they might get 10 percent off. On the fifth visit, it's a buy-one-get-one-free meal deal. As the customer returns, the incentives increase in value: free dessert, free appetizer, etc.

- **Coupons for the next visit.** It's the boomerang effect. They each come in and leave with a coupon for their next visit. It has a psychological effect on customers: a coupon is like cash they want to spend, but it's good only at your business, not your competitors'. When the time comes for another night out for dinner, they'd rather save with you than spend more at a similar competitor's.

- **Fix your mistakes.** It happens, like it or not. An order is wrong. A server abandons your customer for too long, or the atmosphere is just plain ruined. What do you do? Show goodwill. Give him an "on the house" invitation to come back and try again sometime. He won't turn down the free meal. And when he returns, make sure the best server takes care of him.

Have Hotels Promote Your Restaurant

Where do out-of-towners find out where to dine whenever they come to town and stay in a local hotel? From the hotel itself! Many visitors prefer to go out and experience the local fare rather than stay stuck in their room ordering from the hotel's room service. Remember, most hotels have the Yellow Pages in each room, but many will even partner with local restaurants to promote specific places as a courtesy to their guests. Here are two ways you can get visitors into your place using hotel hype:

- **Have the hotel put you in its special directory.** Often times, hotel concierges will have a special entertainment and dining reference list for their guests. Ask them if they can add your name to the list.

- **Give them brochures or menus.** Many hotels have a stack of menus in each room for visitors to peruse and determine where they want to go or order in from. Make sure that they have plenty on hand in case some get ruined or misplaced. Offer to prepare a binder for the hotel with your menu in the first position, of course.

Going After Groups

Customers often have problems finding restaurants that can accommodate larger groups. Even groups of 12 sometimes find themselves turned away or waiting for long periods of time if they don't have reservations beforehand. And what about those really large groups, such as wedding parties or reunions? They like to hold their festivities at restaurants too! So how do you cater to these groups and others who might bring in tons of business, without spending major advertising dollars? Like this:

- **Make it a well-known fact.** Spread the word that you have the space and the willingness to host a party of 12 or more, up to whatever number you can legally house.

- **Approach specific groups.** Is there a chapter of Toastmasters in the area? Contact their representative to let him or her know that you're willing to play host for the event. Do this for all organizations you think would make good clients.

- **Arrange a set price and offer a limited menu to larger parties.** This keeps their cost down somewhat. But it also makes it easy for your culinary staff and waitstaff to prepare ahead of time.

- **Print up the facts.** Although a phone call is a nice effect, it probably won't work two months down the road, when a group is looking for a place to gather and can't remember your business name.

- **Brochures.** Use a software program, such as Microsoft Publisher, to print a brochure yourself that tells customers who you are, where you're located and what kinds of deals you offer to larger groups in the area. Or, use a professional freelance design service, such as Megadesign, www.mega-designs.com.

- **Set aside space just for them.** Large groups are usually very boisterous (even the tamest of crowds get noisy from time to time). You don't want to turn them off by asking them to keep it down. Also, don't ruin the other patrons' night by seating them within earshot of a crowd of 50-plus excited people.

- **Give them special attention.** When you host a large party, give them their own servers. Don't have the servers trying to accommodate the party and other guests.

- **Book business meetings.** Many corporations have several conference rooms, but oftentimes they're already booked up when a last-minute meeting of executives is called. Make it known that you can accommodate these groups. Go out and visit these organizations.

- **Design a designated driver campaign.** When groups of people come out for a night, offer free drinks (nonalcoholic) to the designated driver of each group.

Music Makes the World Go Round

While cocktail hour is no place for a live band, music can have a dramatic effect on your business if it's used the right way at the right time. Back in the late '80s, a restaurant called, simply, Sam's was well known for holding in the summer what was marketed strictly by word-of-mouth as a "Sam's Jam." Sam's had a great big parking lot. Once or twice a month, on the weekend, they'd close it off and have a "battle of the bands" contest. Did they pay for the music? Nope. Did they ring up a lot of food and alcohol sales? You bet! People came early and stayed late! The bands wanted exposure. They were prescreened to make sure they were talented enough to entertain the crowd, and then the rest was up to them! Here are some music dos and don'ts to help your promotional appeal soar:

- **DO test a live band ahead of time.** You don't want a heavy metal hair band entertaining a jazz crowd (or vice versa).

- **DON'T hire a band for slow or cocktail hours.** Use bands when the crowd is up for a musical event and whenever there are lots of people wanting to have a good time. You don't want musicians playing to an empty room.

- **DO let the customers sing for themselves!**
Karaoke is a fun alternative to paying for a
band. A one-time investment in a karaoke
machine is smart if you plan to use it a lot. But
you might want to rent one the first few times to
see if your crowd is the type to brave it and belt
out tunes of their own. Karaoke machines may
be purchased at
www.karaokecenter.com/equipment.htm and
www.acekaraoke.com.

- **DON'T charge your customers an admission
or cover fee unless the performers are well
known in the area.** If this is their first gig and
they bomb, your customers aren't going to be
very happy having to pay for a poor
performance.

Daily Specials That Sparkle with Delight

Daily specials are a great boomerang incentive that
keeps your customers coming back - on a regular
basis! You can implement these no matter what fare
you serve, or at what time of day. Breakfast, lunch
and dinner can all have daily specials. People come to
rely on them and like knowing that their favorites will
be served at a special rate on a day they know ahead
of time. Here are several daily special ideas that you
can use to boost sales and increase repeat customer
count:

- **Enchilada Mondays.** Use a specific dish that
appeals to your customers – one that's requested
more often than all of the others – and then offer
it at a reduced rate on one day of the week. You

can even choose to run a very small ad that day in the paper that mentions the daily special.

- **Spread the word.** Don't just serve your regular menu: make sure customers see a table tent that shows your daily specials for the entire week. It's good for your waitstaff to memorize these, so if a customer asks, they'll know the special for each and every day. Print your own by using software such as Menu Pro available at www.atlantic-pub.com, or order them at www.armsco.com.

- **Don't mix them up.** Don't serve enchiladas on Monday one week and then on Thursday the next. Customers want reliability, so make sure you keep consistent.

- **Take out what's not working.** If you see a crowd for Enchilada Monday, but nobody is ordering Waldorf salad on Wednesdays, then you might need to rethink the daily special for that particular day. Ask the waitstaff and chef what they think would go over well.

Catering to Kids

Many restaurants don't cater to children simply because the ambiance isn't right for young people. Yet many food industry professionals love pleasing the kids – and for good reason! Kids nag. Worse than parents, they nag until they're blue in the face: "Mommy, I wanna go there for dinner!" Many parents who are seeking a night away from the stove will oblige their kids' wishes just to get a little peace of mind that the kids will be happy and, therefore, out of their hair for awhile. Here are some kid-friendly ideas you can use too:

- **Crayons!** They're cheap, and so are blank printable kids' pictures you can get right off the Internet. Every time a party comes in with kids, you give them about four crayons and a blank picture to keep them busy. Then, either give it to them to take home or enter it in your "kid coloring contest" for a free dessert that month! Order the crayons direct at www.crayola.com.

- **Comfort!** Kids can't sit still for very long. Also, that length of time is even shorter if your seats are hard and uncomfortable. Either put them in a booth (kids love booths), or make sure they have an area away from other patrons who might be bothered by the little ones.

- **Shapes!** Chicken nuggets the shape of a monster or french fries covered in the new purple ketchup. A fried-egg face with bacon eye brows and hash-browns hair. You get the idea. It's a good idea to cater to both boys and girls: one gender tends to like the weird and wacky and the other to appreciate pretty and dainty things.

- **Toys!** Aside from the crayons and pictures, you can offer each child a trip to the treasure box on his or her way out the door. Stock the treasure box with items you get in bulk at the dollar store - and be sure to mix dolls with bugs, or else half are likely to be put off by the selection!

Fascination with Freebies

Something for nothing! This is perhaps one of the greatest concepts on the face of this Earth. Find a way to give it to your customers, and you'll find them coming back again and again. There are tons of ways you can do this, but let's take a look at some of the most effective freebie promotions:

- **FREE kids' meals.** You can do this one of two ways: one free kids' meal with every adult purchase or free kids' meals, period. Many restaurants prominently display "Kids eat free" promotional signs on the windows of their establishments. If you don't like feeding people for free all of the time, then you might do it for one night only: "Tuesdays, kids eat free."

- **FREE dessert for the birthday boy or girl.** Yes, even grown-ups like getting a free piece of cake on special occasions. Some restaurants even give out free small, whole cakes - large enough for each person at the table to get a taste.

- **FREE tickets to a local event.** Many events are free, anyway, and you can hand out the tickets with every meal as an added incentive. If possible, stamp one side of the ticket with a discount stamp offering them 10 percent off their next visit.

- **FREE meal if...** Many fast-food restaurants offer the order free of charge if the employee fails to give a receipt with the meal. You can come up with a similar incentive to keep your customers happy and your waitstaff on their toes. For instance, "Free dessert if we fail to tell you our special for the day!" This way, you've got the customers' attention (they're watching to see if the server messes up), and they'll listen to an added personalized promotion from the house! Another thought: How about messing up on purpose to give away a few free desserts?

Business Card Brouhaha

The business card is a great gimmick that can reap major rewards if you design it the right way - so that it becomes a staple in the wallet of your customer. The problem is that many restaurants don't use them as a handout to their clients – which is a big mistake. Business cards aren't only for professionals in the legal or medical profession to use. They're a miniature version of a more expensive form of advertising and promotion. Here are some ways to use your business card as a special, yet small, publicity package:

- **Turn it into a billboard.** If you had the budget to spend hundreds or thousands of dollars putting up billboards all over town, how would you design it? It doesn't have to be a standard business card with all the usual boring information on it. A billboard business card can be anything that you want it to be.

- **Be bold.** On your business card put catchy phrases, tag lines or offers in bold print. You want certain text to stand apart from other items.

- **Make it a cut above the rest.** To make your business card stand apart from the crowd, you need to construct it differently. Make it smaller or larger than a normal business card, or better yet, have a printer design it in a very unusual way – as an animal or a piece of food. Print it on a CD-ROM; business card CDs are a great way to get your message across to clients and prospects. These CDs fit in most CD drives and have room for 50 MB of data: enough for sound, video and text. In quantities of 1,000 or more, they cost less than $1.50 each. Check out www.diskduper.com/bizcard.htm or www.global-rendering.com/cdrom.

- **Texture tips you can use.** Another great way to make your business card an unusual addition to your customers' collections is to have it textured in a very odd way. Go to the extreme: have it smooth as silk, grainy or zigzagged - something to add a cool effect to help them remember your name.

- **Make it a miniature menu.** You can create a business-card-size business card, but actually turn it into a miniature fold-out menu! On the inside and back of the card, you can either focus on certain elements, such as appetizers and desserts, or list your daily specials. In a hurry to order your business cards? Check out www.businesscardsfast.com.

Paperwork Packages to Promote Your Restaurant

Most people don't realize the importance of branding everything that goes out their door with their logo or other promotional pieces on it. Even items that you know will be thrown away at a later date, or even within minutes, should be considered marketing tools that you can use. There are other ways to make certain paper items a staple fixtures in office buildings and in homes all over the city. How many times have you received a pizza promotional magnet for your refrigerator? It's one of the first places that people look when figuring out what to eat for dinner, so what better positioning than directly on the front of the fridge? Here are some ways you can use paper promotions and keep your name in front of the public:

- **Rolodex card additions.** If your restaurant is one that frequently meets the needs of company lunch crowds, why not give them free handouts to add to their Rolodexes? They can come in handy when a secretary is given a demand to plan a last-minute luncheon for numerous executives who are working through lunch. Also, consider using a brightly colored tab so that your card stands out from the rest and is easy to find.

- **Do a postcard campaign.** Postcard campaigns are a great way to approach your local customers in a very cost-effective manner. All you have to do is buy prestamped postcards from your local post office and use your own printer to print a campaign to send out. Your local chamber of commerce can help you with a list of businesses in your area, and you can include a coupon on the postcard to get them in the door!

- **Start a newsletter.** You can let people opt into your newsletter by filling out their name and mailing address on a comment card. In the newsletter, you can highlight all of the upcoming events and entertainment news for your city. Always, of course, include a nice, big ad (with or without coupon) for your restaurant. Use your Web site to collect e-mail addresses for an electronic version of your newsletter; the benefit is that it will cost you nothing to mail out 100 or 100,000.

- **Print those "to go's."** If your restaurant is one where people often come in and get "to go" order, then be sure to print those bags, or other packages, with promotional coupons or menus they can use again and again. Provide a marked parking space for take-out customers, or consider a drive-thru window. Consider a delivery person. Make it easy for your customers to access the service.

Cross-Promotional Possibilities

You don't have to be at war with your competitors. Sometimes it's a good idea to partner with other retailers in the area to offer a combination approach to marketing to the locals. Cross-promotions are a way of pairing up with someone else to share costs of campaigning, and both profit from the results. You have to figure out what goes well with your fare.

You've no doubt ordered a pizza and seen a movie rental coupon on the cover of the pizza box. Likewise, many movie rental outlets have stacks of coupons for pizza readily available for their customers. Here are some other ways to partner up and cross-promote your business:

- **Movie and dinner.** Most of the time when couples go out for a night, they plan on dinner and a movie. Why not approach the local movie theaters and see if they'll offer a $1-off coupon to your customers if you do the same for theirs?

- **Kids' toy stores.** Depending on whether or not your company caters to the little ones, you might be able to join up with a local "Toys R Us," or other establishment to offer a coupon, and vice versa.

- **Local theme park attractions.** Six Flags, water parks, and Disney theme parks: all of them advertise on soda cans, flyers, food coupons - you name it. Get in on the action and work out a deal to hand out season pass discount coupons to your customers in exchange for one of their campaigns being printed with your advertisement or coupon.

- **Tagalong opportunities.** Know of another business in the area that has a frequent-buyer program or discount card? Many supermarkets have space for printed coupons on the back of their receipts where other local businesses can promote their specials. Also consider theater and movie tickets.

Turn Your Restaurant into Tourist Central

Tourist dollars can really add up - but not just for local theme parks and highly established attractions. You can grab a piece of the tourist dollar as well, if you follow our nine easy steps to marketing to the out-of-towners:

- **Taxicab consideration.** Pamper your taxicab drivers and they'll be glad to recommend your restaurant to all of their passengers. Give them a spill-proof mug to drive with, complete with your logo on it, and offer them coupon cards and miniature menus to hand out to their passengers. Whenever their customers bring in five coupons, the cab driver gets a mailing for a free meal!

- **Concierge as a PR candidate.** Turn the concierge into your friend, and you'll find a flurry of patrons coming through your door. They are the direct source of where-to-eat recommendations for thousands of visitors every year.

- **Stay abreast of convention news.** If your city is large enough to be the host of numerous conventions throughout the year, then you need to be a part of that! Find out which groups are scheduled to come through town, then contact the organization directly and offer to provide coupons and miniature menus to their attendees.

- **Pillow mints.** Isn't it nice when you stay out of town to find a nice mint on your pillow, where the maid has turned down your blanket for you? Why not have mints printed with your logo on them and give them away to area hotels to give to their guests? Get your personalized chocolates at www.branders.com, www.hospitalitymints.com or www.igopromos.com/personalized_candies.html.

- **Door hangers.** If the hotel doesn't already have "Do Not Disturb" hangers, then you might offer to provide them free - as long as you can have your logo and phone number printed on them. For one source, visit www.hotelamenities.co.za/ Roomsign.asp.

- **Entertainment booklets.** Many out-of-towners who live in-state buy coupon booklets for when they travel in-state. You should post a discount ad in these booklets, because those patrons have actually spent money to receive the discounts in the first place.

- **Chambers of commerce.** There's no better way to network than to advertise in their publications and join their group. Travelers often go directly to, or otherwise contact, the chamber of commerce just to get advice on what area businesses are recommended. Sign up with an international force at www.chamber-of-commerce.com.

- **Airline meals.** A new airline in Texas allowed a local chef to cater the meals on their flights. Some airlines even have kids' meals from some of the favorite fast-food chains in the country. Strike a deal, and you may be the best airline food in the sky!

- **Bus patrons in.** If there is a local airport that has a large number of hotels on-site, you can offer shuttles once or twice a night to and from the restaurant for people who don't have rental cars while in town.

Promoting Your Place of Business Online

The Internet is a gold mine for business. Advertising, promotion and publicity are dirt cheap, and you have access to a worldwide audience. What could be better? If you're not online, you're not in anymore! Everyone has a Web site, and you can even make one for free! Need a professional Web site designer that works inexpensively and specializes in the hospitality field? Contact www.gizwebs.com or by e-mail at gizweb@shawus.com. Here are eight virtual tips you can use to boost sales and build your name on the Net:

- **Search-engine submission.** If you don't submit your URL to search engines, your site will never be found! Go to www.dmoz.com and submit your site once. This way, your information will spider over to various other search engines, including all of the major ones!

- **Ad banners.** You can place banners on relevant sites where you think your name should be placed and pay only when customers actually click on it to come to your site. Or, get paid for hosting other companies on your site at www.hitcents.com.

- **Local Web site partnerships.** In most large cities, there is a main city Web site where local businesses are encouraged to advertise or place their banners.

- **Global audience.** Attract incoming tourists by advertising your site on tourist Web sites, such as www.travelocity.com. Also, get listed on all the free reservation sites. Key in "Restaurant Reservations" in any search engine and start signing up your restaurant.

- **Take orders online.** On your Web site, have an order form that alerts you whenever an incoming take-out order comes in.

- **Start an e-commerce section online.** The Hard Rock Café and others have a special area where they sell merchandise, like hats, T-shirts and more, online. It's a great way to get your logo spread all around the world! Some restaurants ship their salad dressings, sauces, breads and ribs all over the world.

- **E-mail advertising.** Auto responders are a way to capture the e-mail of your visitors and then court them into your business by sending out occasional publicity promos via e-mail. The system does it for you: all you have to do is get their e-mail addresses, which can be done on a customer comment card.

- **Newsletter spots.** Know of an online newsletter that has thousands of recipients? Then you can pay to place a mention of your business in it for very little, if anything! Many of these newsletters offer some sort of trade, like a banner on your site.

Marketing Mechanics That Work!

Sometimes simplicity is key when you're trying to discover new ways of marketing to the public mind-set. Here are five more ways that you can promote your business and make the most out of your publicity opportunities.

- **Loss items.** Snag their attention with a $0.99 chicken sandwich at lunch, but then have everything else full price. Not everyone will want the chicken sandwich, and they'll still be paying full price for their drinks and side items. It's a great way to get new customers in or to promote a new menu item.

- **USP.** Every business should have a Unique Selling Position. The lowest prices. The best seafood. Can't get it anywhere else. All of these are USPs that position you as the only place to go for the goods customers want. Need help coming up with one? The pros at www.elance.com can help you out.

- **Customer survey.** If you have access to their mailing addresses, send a longer survey to each customer to find out what it is customers like and don't like about your restaurant. What would they like to see changed? Added? Removed?

- **Partnering locations.** You can join food-service programs all over the city. Schools now serve fast food; corporations have cafeterias that might serve your fare; theme parks, ball parks and nursing homes have special needs too! You will need to get on their bid lists.

- **Kiosk convenience.** If they won't come to you, then you go to them. Roll a kiosk out to a busy area at lunchtime. Or, drive a meal car to their location. Consider adding a delivery staff. Construction workers will especially appreciate the service!

Daring promotions are the kind that get noticed.

CHAPTER THREE

DARING PUBLICITY STUNTS TO JUMP-START YOUR BUSINESS

How Daring?

There's a saying that goes, "There's no such thing as bad publicity." Well, that may be true in the eyes of Hollywood, but in the real world, public opinion wields a lot of power! A hepatitis breakout or food poisoning epidemic is definitely not good PR. But there is a way to start what appears to be a negative campaign and magically transform it into something fun for the whole community. Read on to learn more:

- **Be bold.** One of the best ways to boost your business is to get a little daring in your approach. What kinds of promotions generally catch the eye of the public and the media? Those that are totally off the wall!

- **Publicize your stunts.** Even if the big three media don't pick up on your gimmicks, you can rest assured that you'll still get plenty of great coverage. How?

- **Word of mouth** - a very compelling incentive for people to visit your establishment. If their friends brag about your restaurant or people begin talking about it in general, then others will likely bring it up in a conversation with at least ten other people.

- **The water cooler.** If you're being outrageous, then the water cooler will be a hot area of conversation for people all wanting to know if the others have heard about your little stunt.

Declare War on Your Competitors

Everyone loves a good spat - especially if it's all done in good, clean fun. The key is not to let anyone know ahead of time that what you plan on starting is already known and agreed upon by the other guy. If they know beforehand that it's a hoax, then their interest level dwindles, and the fun is ruined. You're seeking shock value, an "I can't believe they did that!" kind of response. Then, once the community begins taking sides, with each of you fighting for their loyalty, you let the cat out of the bag slowly to reveal that you're really having fun with your competition. The following are some tips to help you wage war on the other guys:

- **Strike a deal.** You don't want to launch a "fun" war without the consent of the other party. Find another similar restaurant willing to go along with the plan - someone willing to go all out and enjoy the attention you'll be getting, without letting things take a turn for the worst.

- **Draw up a plan.** It's good to have a written proposal to give to the other manager or owner so that there are no surprises to either party. It might be fun to agree to do a few minor surprises, as long as it's not damaging to the other party to a large degree.

- **Have a time line.** Each phase of the "war" should happen at just the right time - possibly whenever the public is planning their dining strategy for the weekend. Do it on Monday, and people might forget by the time Friday and Saturday nights roll around.

- **Get the press involved.** If you're planning a fun event, send a press release ahead of time to invite the media to cover it. Maybe host a contest between the restaurants, where the employees go up against each other in a wacky race.

- **Let the battle begin.** Depending on your warring strategy, you'll want to have dibs on who starts the feud in the public eye. It might be best if the other guy starts it, or vice versa.

- **Be vocal about it.** Instead of saying you're the best burger joint in town, start using slogans that read, for example, "Better than Bob's Burgers." Of course, Bob will be doing the same, but all in good fun.

- **Get the customers involved.** Start giving away or selling funny feuding bumper stickers, pins and/or T-shirts. You also can give away a free dessert to customers who have a picture of themselves wearing the T-shirt at a certain local landmark.

- **Magnetic trade-ins.** Do you happen to have a magnet on your refrigerator of your favorite pizza parlor? Have a trade-in promotion where customers who trade in a competitor's magnet for one of yours get a discount coupon. Order yours at www.maitland.bmr.com.au/accolades/magnets.htm.

- **Rip up the Yellow Pages!** You can cut the competition out of the race by giving away a coupon to patrons who bring in your competitor's ad - cut out of their phone book.

Wacky, Off-the-Wall Promos

Sometimes you have to go to extremes to win the war of publicity stunts galore. Some famous bar and grills are known for having customers hang items of clothing, or dance and sing, on the counter of the bar. Here are several ways you can grab your piece of the promotional pie by doing the unexpected and shocking your customers into satisfaction:

- **Skating around the room.** Sonic isn't the only restaurant to have waitresses and waiters skating around the parking lot. If you're willing to take the risk, have your servers skate around while they serve up fare day and night.

- **Hacking the suits.** Hate the boring, stuffy crowds that sometimes find their way into your restaurant? Some places will actually cut off a man's tie – if he dares wear one inside – and hang it as a trophy on the wall behind the bar.

- **Serenades for the sweet.** Is your restaurant a place where couples come to have intimate dinner conversation? Hire a singer to serenade them while they dine. Walking around the room to sing to each couple is an added bonus!

- **Shoe-shine shaper-uppers.** Lunchtime business crowds will appreciate having an old-fashioned shoe-shine stand ready to keep them on their toes before they return to the nine-to-five drudge.

- **Full-moon freak-out.** Know of a full moon coming up soon? Plan a promo where diners are invited to an especially freaky night of fun. Servers can even dress up as werewolves for added fun!

- **Leap-year lowdown.** It can happen only once every four years, so pump up the publicity around your Leap Year Lawn Party, where the restaurant is turned inside out for a night!

Hold a Kissing Contest

This is a perfect promotion for Valentine's Day, but you can also hold it at any time of the year to promote love and coupling among the frisky crowd. Holding a kissing contest usually requires a rather large prize, so first you'll have to try to sign on a major contributor. Try the following tactics:

- **Draft a proposal to give to local manufacturers.** Find out if they'd be interested in giving away a medium-to large-sized prize to one lucky couple that kiss the longest. The local news will probably report live toward the beginning and end of the promotion, just to check in with the lip-weary couple, so expect some great media coverage!

- **Send the winners to Kissimmee, Florida.** The grand prize might be a trip to KISSimmee, Florida. But you can also find another prize if you can't find a sponsor for the trip. Learn more about this vacation destination at www.floridakiss.com.

- **Don't forget the runners up.** All that kissing is bound to be tiring, so be sure to award some sort of prize to those who don't last the longest. Prizes can range from free meals to T-shirts and an assortment of other small prizes.

Eat Like a Cow - Don't Look Like One Promo

Now, it may sound rude to insinuate that people are overweight - but let's face it, with the diet industry bringing in over $33 billion each year in the United States, we already know it! People are craving health and fitness - almost as much as they are craving cookies and carbs! How can you help them lose weight and stay fit, while still bringing them into the restaurant for food and fun? Easy! All you have to do is bring healthier-eating options to your restaurant. Be sure to tell people about it. Contact your local food editor and the paper. Send flyers to local fitness centers to spread the word. Also consider the following opportunities:

- **Vegetarian menu options.** The vegetarian craze is more popular than ever. If you can offer even a couple of vegetarian meals, your customers will appreciate it more than you know. Be sure to offer the various forms: some vegetarians won't even eat dairy products, so try to please them all.

- **Weight Watchers specials.** Try to keep up with the various diet specials going on. For instance, Weight Watchers has a point system. Why not get a Weight Watchers employee to evaluate your meals for "Points" value and then add that information to your menu? They'll be sure to tell their members about it too!

- **Carbs versus no carbs.** Another fitness craze is between the Carb Addicts and Carb Avoiders, so you can serve special options for customers who want to stack their plates full of carbohydrates and those who want to steer clear of them.

- **Get into the Zone.** Celebrities and affluent people are paying hundreds of dollars every week just to have Zone meals delivered to their homes. It's one of Hollywood's hottest diet crazes in existence, so many of your customers will be thrilled to find these options on your menu! Learn more at www.zoneperfect.com.

- **The half-plate special.** It's been estimated that the average size of a meal has more than doubled over the past decade. Even plate sizes have grown from 9 inches to 12.5 inches. Offer your customers a half-size special to cut down on their caloric intake.

- **Let them graze.** Most weight-loss success stories show that those people eat healthy snacks before dinner to help them lose weight. Offer healthy appetizers as an option to boost sales and promote the fitness of your customers.

Radical Reader Awards

Reading is one of the top priorities for American educators all across the nation. Many restaurants, such as Pizza Hut, sponsor reading programs encouraging and enticing young people to read more books. Below are a few ways you can jump on the bandwagon and help make reading a number-one priority for the young people in your area as well:

- **Post their progress.** When you launch a reading campaign, be sure to notify the participants that somewhere in your restaurant, their names and progress will be displayed for all to see. This will not only encourage them to read more to beat the competition, but also to come back often to see how well they're doing against the others!

- **Milestone surprises.** After every ten books they read (or you pick a number), they'll get a free sundae or kids' meal. Pizza Hut allows readers to set their own goals, and once they've met them, the kids get free personal-size pizzas.

- **The big winner.** Set a big winner for each age group. You might be able to get a major book chain to contribute several gift certificates from their establishment to give away as prizes.

Let Your Customers In on Your Secret Recipes

You can start a promotion where you actually teach your customers the secrets that they've always wanted to know about your tasty pot roast and your succulent lamb chops. We're not talking the exact Kentucky Fried Chicken recipe, but you can always show them a little bit of what they would like to know. Here are some ideas to get you going:

- **Hold a cooking class.** Have your chef or a professional independent chef come in to show some of your clients how to cook the dishes that they love best. Consider offering classes on how to cook a heart-healthy version of the menu items. Your classes can be off-hours, so they don't interfere with other business.

- **Show them how to prepare a fine-dining experience.** Many people would love to know how to hold a formal dinner party. You can have your customers come in before the dinner shift and show them how to fold napkins into swans, how to position silverware and prepare elaborate garnishes and teach them how to design a beautiful centerpiece.

- **Let them eat cake - and cook it too!** Cake-decorating classes have gained in popularity and are a fun, interactive way to get to know your customers. You can have them prepare the cakes to take home and invite their entire family in for a slightly discounted meal.

- **Taste of the world.** There are some charities that hold "Taste of the World" campaigns, but you can do it right in-house. You can either send out invitations to attract customers to a special event, or offer it to everyone who comes in. Set up a special menu with appetizers, main entrees and desserts from every corner of the world! This is especially fun if you put your own personal twist on the idea and make it unusual in presentation and style. Also consider wine-tasting nights, champagne nights and cigar nights.

Position Yourself As a Promotion

If you've been in the industry for a long period of time, or even if you've become a success in a relatively short period of time, you can position yourself as an expert. Launch some promotion for your business by selling your expertise. Consider the following:

- **Contact your local television stations.** Local TV stations, especially in larger metroplex areas, like to have someone in certain industries they can call on to provide weekly updates to their audience. For instance, there's usually a doctor who checks in on one or more days of the week to offer health and medical news. Why not approach the station director with some ideas you have on ways to promote food and dining news for your area?

- **Do the same with your local paper.** If you're from a larger city, you've probably noticed an entire food section that comes out midweek and in the Sunday edition of the paper. You can write a sample column and submit it to the food editor on spec, which means if they like it, they'll publish it. If you're lucky enough to get a column out of it, you'll have free publicity on a continual basis.

Turn Hollywood

Hollywood is a fascination to almost everyone, including men, women and children of all ages. For decades, we've been glued to the television to tune in to our favorite stars in order to see what they're wearing, where they go and whom they're dating. Cash in on this fascination:

- **Have your waiters and waitresses dress up like famous people.** Give them a selection so that they don't show up in something that might be considered distasteful by your customers. Some options could be singers, movie stars, sitcom personalities or even animated stars! Order costumes at www.costumeuniverse.com.

- **Go back in time for a spell.** Take your interior back in the past. Have servers dress up as people from the '20s, '50s, '60s, '70s or even the '80s. Don't stop there, though! Turn the atmosphere into another decade as well, complete with music from another place in time.

- **Get your customers involved.** Advertise the fact that Friday is Fifties Night, Tuesday is Twenties Night, or Saturday is Sixties Night. Have customers dress up to win a prize or get a discount on their meal.

Play Games with Your Customers

Games are a blast for any operation. In everything from fine-dining to fast-food restaurants, everyone likes to experience the possibility of winning something. Even small prizes are a great way to brighten a customer's day. McDonald's uses a Happy Meal. So does almost every other fast-food chain in America. The kids look forward to the toy - even more so than the fries and nuggets. Adults never outgrow their desire to open a little bag and find a prize. Most people grew up with Cracker Jacks, where even a small, thin packet of fake tattoos was enough to cause excitement when the box was empty. Here are some additional ways to play games with your customers and make them happy with their meal:

- **Who Wants to Be a Millionaire for a day?** You can play this very popular trivia game with your customers! Set up a hot seat and have questions created from an Internet search. You can make it so that the level of winnings increases with correct answers: a discount coupon, first level; a buy-one-get-one-free coupon, second level; a free dessert or appetizer, third level; and a completely free meal as the main winning prize. Or, get a local business to kick in some major prizes.

- **Hands-on-the-car games.** Choose any variation of this game. The premise is to make people endure a long period of time to win a major prize. Sometimes you can get a car manufacturer to donate a car for the big win, which will obviously result in tons of publicity for your restaurant.

- **Survivor promo**. Regardless of whether or not this popular reality show continues on a path to success, customers will have a blast being voted off the island and winning a big prize. This is best played with a fun crowd in a very entertaining and lively atmosphere. Let the audience vote in the end for the big winner, and ask the contestants to answer questions to determine who gets voted off throughout.

- **Treasure chest keys.** Get a "treasure chest" with dozens of fake keys and one key that fits a vehicle of some sort. It could be a lawn mower, a jet ski or even a beautiful jewelry box.

- **Mystery envelope promos.** Give your patrons sealed envelopes, with coupons inside, which they can't open until their next visit. When they return, have the server open it at the table to find out what kind of discounts or freebies they'll win.

Have a Pajama Party

Well, not an overnight party – but you can still cater to the night owls and stay open late, especially on weekends, to allow the after-hours crowd a place to hang out and enjoy themselves before they go home. Here are a couple of ways to bring in the late-nighters and keep them up until the sun shines through:

- **Late-night nibbling.** Offer a special promo where you set up a buffet (so that the kitchen can begin shutting down) while patrons enjoy the buffet in the bar area. That way, with a bartender and one or two servers on board, the rest of the place can wind down, while those who are still wound up can keep going.

- **Offer a half-price picnic.** Often, there is a lot of food left over at the end of the night. Why not try to sell out of it before the doors close? Offer half-price specials to customers who come in after a certain hour, such as 10 p.m. Do this for one hour before closing time. Offer a late-night, after-club or theatre menu.

Hold Your Own World Series

The World Series is second only to the Super Bowl in its popularity, and in many instances, it's a bigger event because of its duration. Capitalize on the World Series. Hold an event that gets the attention of the press and puts the spotlight on you. Here are a couple of suggestions:

- **Home-run hopefuls.** Start publicizing that you are going to hold a World Series against your competition (goad them into it if you have to), and then rent the local ball field to host the event, where you'll have stands set up to serve your own fare and sell souvenirs.

- **Logoize your equipment.** Make sure, since you're hosting the event, that all baseballs are emblazoned with your logo. Sell or give away T-shirts with the same and have your logo printed on all of the plastic cups where drinks are sold at the stands.

Dance the Night Away

Dances are falling by the wayside. It was a regular occurrence when we were in middle and high school, but once we become adults, we only fondly remember the days of boogying about. Turn your establishment into a dance parlor for a night, or after regular dining hours: include tables where dancers can rest in between songs and order up some of your delicious fare. You can also charge entry to the extravaganza if you want to. Or, maybe try one of the following ideas:

- **Hold a theme night.** It could be based on the type of music, such as disco, country, or rock. Consider allocating a night based on an idea, such as Family Dance Night or Singles, Widowed or Divorced Dance Night.

- **Have your servers dance too.** Ever been to a '50s-style fast-food place? Many of the servers wear roller skates and dance around to the music blaring from the speakers.

- **Decorate in the past.** Antiques can be expensive, but you can buy old-fashioned decorations for practically nothing by contacting an outlet store or going online and ordering in bulk. Go to www.ebay.com.

*Strive to
ensure customer
satisfaction.*

CHAPTER FOUR

PAMPERING PROMOTIONS TO PACK 'EM IN

Show Your Customers That You Really Care about Their Comfort

Going out to eat doesn't have to be a stressful event, but oftentimes that's what customers experience. They save their money to be able to go out for a relaxing evening where someone else cooks dinner and cleans up afterwards, only to be greeted by a rude waiter, wrong orders and long delays. Earn yourself a reputation for pampering your customers. Bear in mind the following:

- **Publicize the fact that you're looking out for your customers.** Strive to ensure their satisfaction and help them de-stress from the hectic lives that people are prone to live today. Subtle lighting, fresh flowers and comfortable furnishings all publicize the fact that you care about your customers' well-being.

- **Figure out what types of pampering appeal to patrons.** Take your lead from local spas and specialty services. Capitalize on them. Don't think you have to limit yourself to pampering women only.

- **Indulge your clientele with a little TLC.**
Parents, kids, singles and just about everyone
could use a little TLC now and then. Impress
and amaze your guests with a genuinely caring
approach. It never fails - especially when they're
really not expecting it. Get it into their heads
that your establishment is their favorite friendly
restaurant!

Give the Kids Their Own Dining Area

Kids are wild - even the good ones. Therefore, it's
imperative that you know how to handle them in
a fun way so that customers who don't have children
aren't bothered by the noise and fidgeting that kids
almost always bring to the table. Why not give them
their own area to dine in, where they're monitored
and cared for while the parents enjoy a relaxing
evening to themselves? The kids won't feel like they're
being sectioned off. In fact, they'll probably beg to
come back again and again - if you do it right! Try the
following ideas:

- **Bring a babysitter (or two) on board.** Many
teens or young adults would love to earn extra
money babysitting in an environment like this.
In the kids-only area of the restaurant, you can
let the kids eat at smaller tables, order kid-
friendly menu items and play afterwards while
their parents enjoy their meal in peace! You can
also install monitors that will allow parents to
watch their kids at the same time.

- **Design a small-scale activity area.** You can
buy miniature tables, kitchen areas and other

interior designs to create a kid-size restaurant that's separated from the adults.

- **Have a story time.** There are many children's authors who would relish the opportunity to come in and promote their books (and sell autographed copies as well) by reading their stories to the kids. You can also have the babysitters read stories and even have the kids dress up as characters in the stories they read.

- **Have plenty of arts and crafts.** Kids love to play with paints, play dough and anything else they can use to create. Have plenty of smocks to protect their clothing, and keep them occupied by letting them paint pretty pictures for their parents who are dining in another room.

Monthly Spa Extravaganza

Spas are popping up all over the place (including in corporate business offices) to relieve the stress that employees are faced with every day. Americans are working longer hours, and it's taking its toll on family life. People are often reluctant to do anything nice for themselves, so why not do it for them? Bring the spa to your restaurant. Let your customers experience the relaxation techniques many professionals have to offer. Here are a few suggestions you may wish to consider:

- **Get them in the chair.** If your restaurant has hour-long waits and a packed house more often than not, you can turn the frustration of the wait into a positive experience by bringing in a massage therapist to sell 10-minute chair massages for half price. Customers will love the experience, and the massage therapist will make quite a bit of money taking care of your clients each evening.

- **Mother-and-daughter duos.** Why not put your after-hours to good use? Sunday brunch is a great time to hold a mom-daughter spa setup. Corner off one area of your restaurant and allow the pair to get highly discounted (or free) pedicures, manicures, facials or makeovers before the brunch crowd comes in.

- **Don't forget the guys!** Men need therapy too, and many will love being invited to a special dads' day out for a quick shoulder massage before the big game showcases on Sunday.

- **Create a couples' spa setup.** Some guys might be reluctant to take part in the guys-only spa day, so you might have to create a day when women bring their men in and they both have a relaxing day of pampering.

- **Don't forget to feed them.** In ancient Rome, servants used to feed the masters of the house grapes and fan them with feathers. You don't have to go to such extremes, but you may want to offer a light buffet of goodies while they participate in the spa day. Offering fresh fruit, vegetables and dip is a good way to bring their appetite into play.

Pay Back Those Who Always Give to the Community

Ever since September 11, 2001, there has been a renewed interest in and reverence for those who serve and protect our community each and every day. Now more than ever, it's important to show them our appreciation. Below are several ways that you can contribute to the community by showing the police and fire departments, paramedics and military how much they mean to us. Adopt the following considerations:

- **Always offer them a discount.** Many restaurants offer a permanent in-house discount, or at least free beverages, to police officers. Do the same for all of the professionals who protect and serve our country and community.

- **Show your support.** Hang a banner inside or outside of your establishment to show your stripes and honor those who are serving in the military. Hand out bumper stickers or red, white and blue pins for patrons to wear and take home with them.

Notice New Residents

Newcomers often don't know where to go for their dining and entertainment services. Often, they have no friends or relatives in the area to offer them advice on what's good and what's not, so they have to rely on trial and error. Why not step in and become the ambassador to your local area? Take newcomers under your wing. Make them feel right at home. Here are four ways you can play host to your new neighbors and create a hometown atmosphere:

- **Purchase a mailing list.** You can get a specific list that tells you which residents have moved into specific zip codes within a particular time frame. Use these mailing lists to focus on who's new to the area so that you can court them into a visit. Find a specified list at www.caldwell-list.com.

- **Find out about local house closings.** You might be able to partner with your local real estate agencies to have them hand out special invitations to your restaurant to the newcomers to the area. Then, allow them to place their business cards or brochures somewhere in the lobby of your establishment.

- **Mail a freebie.** With your mailing lists, send out a postcard campaign to the new residents to invite them in for a buy-one-get-one-free meal deal. That way, they can bring their spouse or significant other to dine with them.

- **Send a sampler coupon.** If you deliver, you can send a sampler coupon to newcomers to invite them to order delivery service and receive a discount on their first order.

Create a Couple-Friendly Promotion

Aside from families, couples are the second most frequent visitors to your establishment, if not the first. They are out for a night without the kids, or just to enjoy a romantic evening without the stresses of their everyday lives. Why not give them a perfect atmosphere occasionally - something that goes a step beyond the normal night's activities. Advertise it (or better yet, put out a press release) as "Couples Only Night." Here are some suggestions:

- **Melt their hearts.** If you don't normally provide candles, then spring for them; place them on every table and dim the lights. You'll save on energy bills, and the customers will love the ambiance. At www.1partysuppliesandfavors.com, you'll be able to order in bulk and save!

- **Dance the night away.** Get a band - something soft and quiet – and provide a dance area just for the couples. You might even go so far as to invite your customers to attend a second-chance prom night, complete with corsages and up-dos!

- **Make them "Fondue" each other.** Switch the usual fare to a Fondue extravaganza! Couples will love the decadent cuisine and will share in feeding tidbits of cheeses, chocolates and other goodies to each other.

- **Kissing promotion.** At a fancy dinner party, guests are announced upon entry. On special couple promotions, announce each guest with a twist: every time a new couple arrives, the other couples have to kiss.

- **Flatter the ladies with a flower.** Call your local florists to find out if they'll cut you a deal for a regular delivery of flowers. Choose an inexpensive one: the women will eat it up no matter what. Afraid they'll go to waste? Order nice silk ones to hand away! Find them at www.afloral.com.

Beautiful Baby Bash

*Y*ou *gotta see the baaaaaby*, Seinfeld joked on his popular sitcom series in the '90s. All joking aside, babies are built-in brag books that parents love to show off - and the more people who make a big deal out of them, the better! Here are a few ways that you can boost your sales by bringing in the baby brigade. Take one idea, or all of them, and publicize your parenting promotion to the local moms and pops. Consider the following:

- **Beautiful baby prizes.** First of all, make sure every baby wins something in the contest. It's hard to vote for the most beautiful baby, and since you don't want to be the bad guy, let customers vote! You can either hold a live contest or invite parents to post their child's picture on a special bulletin board and on your Web site, where customers can submit ballots for the winner.

- **The three Cs contest.** If you do decide to hold a live contest one night, then have a stage set up with a microphone and hold a crying, cooing and crawling contest as well! First diapered kid to the finish line wins his or her parents a free dinner! Or, give away savings bonds for the kid's future.

- **Be a modeling agency for a day.** See if a local modeling agency might want to hold an audition for new talent at your restaurant! Make it a Saturday or Sunday brunch for beauties!

Harnessing High School Bands

High school bands can be popular attractions, depending on the area you live in and the size and scale of the schools in your district. In fact, many of these high school bands go on to compete in national competitions for bigger recognition. If this is the case in your locale, there are ways you can capitalize on the talent of your neighborhood youth and turn them into dedicated patrons of your restaurant as well. Try the following suggestions:

- **Let them play the lot.** If your parking lot is large enough, invite the band down to play a minishow either to raise funds for one of their trips or just to showcase their talent to the crowd of locals coming to dine.

- **Show the students you value their business.** Kids today have enormous purchasing power. Why not offer a student discount to them to get them in the door and spending dollars to dine with you?

Men Need Extra Attention Too

If you ask anyone on the street what men love most, a large percentage would probably say football. Men love to be pampered and waited on while enjoying the big sporting events that come around in the fall season. Many restaurants offer game-watching promos, but you can take it one step further and pamper them so that each and every Sunday, they and their friends will pack the house to see the game on your TV. Here are a few ideas that might work in your establishment:

- **Give away tickets.** You'd be amazed at how easy it is to get freebies from sports teams' publicity directors. A personal letter almost always gets results. Ask them for a pair of decent seats to give away, and if worse comes to worst, buy one pair and have your patrons fill out a form to win them.

- **Have a free Super Bowl party.** Free snacks, discounted beverages and a big-screen TV will be all you need to get a crowd together for a major event like this.

- **Free buffet during the games.** You can easily set up an inexpensive buffet of snack food and appetizers for patrons to graze on during the Sunday games.

- **Name dishes after key players.** Identify the major players on your home team, and name some dishes after them for the season – or just for Sundays.

- **Guessing games.** You can either buy or get the publicity director to donate jerseys, a signed football and/or a poster, and then have the patrons guess the final outcome of the game. Winner takes all.

The Birthday Club

Birthdays are a staple in special events that people feel the urge to celebrate at a nice restaurant. Nice can mean fancy or fun, just as long as the birthday boy or girl is treated specially, and the entire party is greeted and served with extra attention. Build a computerized database of the information on as many customers as possible. Include birthdays and anniversaries if possible. Below are three ways that you could send the best birthday wishes to your patrons and ensure that every year they'll want to return to celebrate with you:

- **Mail a birthday card.** Send an inexpensive birthday postcard inviting your clients to come in for their celebration, and explain that you'll celebrate by giving them a free meal. Burger King has a Birthday Club for Kids; kids who sign up receive a free kids' meal on their big day.

- **Comp the birthday person's meal.** Either comp the entire meal or drink of his or her choice, but offer some sort of freebie that no one else in the party gets.

- **Let them eat cake.** Provide party hats and other favors to send to the table; when purchased in bulk at a dollar store, they are very cost-efficient. Send out one free piece of cake or an entire small birthday cake, and have the waitstaff sing to the guest of honor. Order them at a discount at www.partysupplydepot.com.

Let the Losers Win for a Change

Nobody likes losing. It bruises our egos and makes us feel down, if only for a fleeting moment. If your state has a lottery, there are ways that you can bring in the thousands of lotto players who live in your area. Listed below are a couple of ways to let "Lotto Losers" have a second chance at success, while cashing in on them at your restaurant:

- **Deduct a losing ticket from your bill.** Many states offer a second-chance sweepstakes, which you can actually play yourself: have people with losing tickets cash them in for a $1 discount on their food bill.

- **Make your own second-chance sweepstakes.** Instead of drawing from a bowl of business cards, have patrons write their name, address and phone number on the back of the losing lotto card and enter it into a weekly second-chance drawing for a special prize. Get a prize donated or buy one yourself.

Spoil the Seniors

Senior citizens love to go out to eat too. But many simply can't do it at the times when specials are usually promoted, such as late night or Happy Hour. Additionally, it's a well-known fact that many seniors watch their spending very carefully, so you have to be able to give them a good deal so that you can compete with the other restaurants ready to offer seniors a discount. Here are a couple of ways you can spoil them rotten and get them returning on a regular basis:

- **Encourage early-bird dining.** Seniors eat out early, because they often go to bed early, so offer a senior discount between 4 and 6 p.m.

- **Offer senior portions.** Many seniors don't want a full-sized meal, and they also don't want to pay for it! Give them a smaller portion with a smaller check, and they'll be happy you did!

Company Promotions to Cheer About

Catering to the local companies will serve your business well. Draft up a letter of introduction to the Human Resources staff to alert them of your existence and to announce that you'll be serving their community and their company in particular. Here are three ways to get the business community investing in your restaurant for years to come:

- **Stuff the payroll.** Send a note to the departmental head of accounting asking if it's okay to mail the department paycheck stuffers that will offer their employees special discount coupons when they come in to dine with you.

- **In-house promotion for another company.** At some area banks, they take one business card from the fishbowl of submissions and allow that business to advertise within the bank for one full month. You can do the same! If a home improvement store wins for the month, allow them to set up a display area promoting their business, and have your POS system print out a discount coupon for use at their store.

- **Put it on a pad.** Have special pads of paper printed with your company name, menu items, take-out phone number and fax number printed on it. Send them to the companies in the area for use by the secretaries. One of the secretaries' responsibilities might be to order lunch for incoming groups and meetings. You can get a good deal at www.giftselection.com/pads.html.

Extra Special Touch Promos

Sometimes the small things in life are what affect us more than big events – someone giving up his seat for you on the bus or paying your bill for you when you're a few dollars short at the grocery store. Listed below are seven ways you can do something extra to promote your restaurant in the eyes of the public:

- **Send out thank-you notes.** They're not just for gift recipients anymore! Personalize a short note to thank groups who hosted a meeting at your restaurant, or to company heads who allowed in-house promotions for their employees.

- **Offer a points program.** Many businesses offer a deal where for every dollar spent, the customer earns one point. Customers can redeem the points at any time. For instance, 300 points gets them a $25 gift certificate. For 10,000 points they get an in-home catered meal! Follow the airlines.

- **Door-to-door dinner program.** Hire a door-to-door marketing company to sell buy-one-get-one free booklets for $20. For the next 20 meals, the customer gets one free meal with one coupon. The catch? The booklet has an expiration date, so all coupons have to be redeemed by then.

- **Recipe secrets.** Put together a special cookbook of your famous recipes, and get the local retail stores to carry it. Travelers coming into Texas, for instance, might be interested in a cookbook on Tex-Mex fare, and while they're in town, they will want to try out the recipes at your location! You can also sell the book in the restaurant.

- **Team sign-up spot.** Do you have a city Little League group in your area? They're always looking for a place to hold their sign-up meetings. Many opt for a kid-friendly fast-food restaurant, and you can be sure the kids won't let mom leave without a kids' meal to boot!

- **Cable television show.** Cable TV isn't as expensive as regular broadcast television. Get your chef a spot of his or her own, and create a local interactive cooking show that makes people recognize your name all over town!

- **Employee buttons.** Bennigan's and T.G.I. Friday's often have their employees wear promotions on their uniforms! A button that says, "Ask me about our special of the day," serves as a reminder for customers that they might get a good deal if they speak up! Order your own personalized buttons at www.pinpromotions.com.

Closed-to-the-Public Special-Event Nights

Just as everyone wants to know the owner, everyone loves to be on the invite-only list for special-event nights. For one evening, close your restaurant to the public and watch the elite come in for a wonderful night on the town. Here are eight ways that you can spice up your special night, including four evenings of fun you can promote to get you started. The public will eat it up! Try the following ideas:

- **Cigar aficionado night.** Cigar smoking isn't just for men anymore! Many women get into the swing of things, and it's a great way to bring in high-dollar clients who appreciate the habit. Order some to hand out at www.egars.com.

- **Wine-tasting event.** A wine-tasting is an event that can cater to people of any income level.

However, it's one that people appreciate as an upscale practice. Bring in a connoisseur to help with the niceties, and you'll have a first-class promotion.

- **Behind-the-scenes tour night.** If your restaurant is a four- or five-star affair, you can host an event where exclusively invited patrons can come in for a night of preparation, indulgence and sampling of exquisite dishes the chef prepares.

- **Fashion-show event.** If you're in a major city, turn your restaurant into a catwalk for a night. Invite those in the industry and the top social names in the area, and you'll have a hit on your hands!

- **Install search lights.** Search lights aren't very expensive to rent, and they can add flair to your event because everyone within miles of you will want to know what the fuss is all about. Find out where you can rent yours at www.lighting4rent.com.

- **Roll out the red carpet - literally!** A red-carpet affair will make patrons feel like they're a part of Hollywood for an evening. Have escorts on hand to meet the single ladies at the curb and walk them into your place of business.

- **Black-tie invitations.** Get your invitations professionally prepared and specify "black tie" to zip up the event a bit. Women will love having a place to wear a new outfit, and everyone will feel special for a few hours.

- **Make them take a second gander.** Unusual staff uniforms are the backbone of Hooters establishments. While you don't have to implement short shorts and barely-there tops, you can use uniforms to get people talking at the water cooler the next day. Get wacky with it and, best of all,make it a fun promotion.

- **Entertainment for the patrons.** For a night like this, you'll want a subtle entertainer to please your guests. Don't opt for a rock-and-roll band this night. Try a jazz or classical band. You might even be able to talk the local college instructor into sending in student performers for practice! Just be sure to screen them beforehand.

- **Lucky lottery promotion.** Give out $1 lottery tickets to each table. You can easily make it up by promoting special desserts and drinks to boost each overall sale.

- **Have a color campaign.** Blue Mondays, Teal Tuesdays, White Wednesdays, etc. Have a promotion where every day of the week is dedicated to a color of the rainbow. Every patron who wears that color shirt gets a discount on his or her meal.

CHAPTER FIVE

WORD-OF-MOUTH PROMOTIONS TO MAKE YOUR SALES SPARKLE

Customer Satisfaction - Unexpected Gestures Guests Will Talk About

There's no stronger publicity than a satisfied customer. There are restaurants that open their doors and sit back while the sales are rung up and pay no attention to whether or not their customers had a satisfying experience. These are the places that open and close their doors within less than two years. Without customer satisfaction, you'll have no chance of survival in the food service industry. So, publicize the fact that your establishment is the tops in providing premium guest services. Follow these guidelines:

- **Politeness.** Insist that all employees are extremely polite, at all times - even under provocation! Stand out from the crowd. Customer service, according to recent surveys, has hit an all-time low. Surveys have shown that people believe rudeness is an all-too-common problem affecting every facet of our public interaction. Every restaurant in the wide spectrum of the food service industry relies on customer satisfaction.

- **Draw on personal experience.** Think about the last time you went out to a new restaurant in your area. Chances are, you immediately determined whether it was a place where customers were treated with care and concern, or a place where the dollar was put before service. Your decision probably affected whether or not you planned on ever returning a second time. If you were ignored, or even just treated mildly, you might be swayed to dine elsewhere next time around. Never forget this sobering fact.

- **Give customers the red-carpet treatment - be attentive.** Give guests a good old-fashioned welcome. Once people know you're one to be counted on, they'll show you their appreciation by frequenting your establishment on a regular basis. It costs nothing to be attentive, and guests will be back again and again. Here are some ways you can impress your guests and make them feel special. Get them talking about the star quality they were given at your place!

- **Offer an "all special requests accepted" policy.** People are generally reluctant to ask for special requests for fear it will irritate the staff or the chef and result in less-than-satisfactory service. Promote the fact that you readily accept special order requests, and people will feel comfortable ordering variations.

- **Put up a sign offering complimentary valet parking.** When people see a sign out front that announces FREE valet parking, they'll come back for the ease of it all. Especially on weekend nights, when customers sometimes wind up walking a block or more to get to the front door, valet parking is a great way to keep people happy. Earn extra revenue by sharing the proceeds with the valet service.

- **Make a big deal out of birthdays.** Many restaurants offer singing servers and a complimentary birthday cake. Go one step above. Tie helium balloons in the birthday person's hair and make them stand on a chair and be sung to by the crowd.

Cash In on Church Organizations

Many churches have after-service get-togethers. Most of the time, they're right on the premises of the church grounds, and the feast is organized by church members themselves and publicized as a potluck supper. But many times, the churchgoers or a smaller group of a very large congregation prefer to go out to dine and relax while they enjoy after-service entertainment. Here are some ways that you can cash in on these festivities:

- **Contact the local church directors.** Send out personalized letters to the leaders of each congregation. Invite them to come to your establishment after Sunday services. Make sure, however, that you understand each religion's policies. For instance, groups like the Seventh-Day Adventists believe it's wrong to dine out on the Sabbath Day, because this causes others to work on a holy day.

- **Offer volume discounts.** Many of these groups can be quite large. Entice them to your establishment by notifying them that you have plenty of room (a banquet area, perhaps). Offer a discount to groups of 20 or more.

- **Cater to the youth groups.** Most churches encourage the youngsters in their congregation to have their very own youth groups. Offer to help raise funds whenever they're in need of additional cash.

Something for Nothing

A little bit of extra attention goes a long way. Offer little extra amenities. People will soon tell their friends and smile about the small gestures that they loved when they visited your establishment. Here are some ways that you can show your customers a little bit of TLC, and get them spreading the word about your pampering environment:

- **Promotional beverages to customers with a long wait.** Have a server ready to offer free small-sized sodas if your customers are forced to wait for long periods of time. It eases their frustration and helps assure them that you care about their needs.

- **Promotional popcorn at the bar.** If you have a bar area where patrons clamor while they wait for a table or enjoy the atmosphere for a few hours, then add a popcorn machine. Hand out bowls or bags full of it. It's a very cheap alternative to pricey nuts. You can order your own machine at www.snappypopcorn.com.

- **Pint-sized portion promotions.** Not everyone wants the huge special with two of everything on their plate. Many patrons simply want a smaller portion of a meal, so offer it to them - at a discounted price, of course.

- **Promote pampering in the ladies' room.** Present a clean bathroom with facial tissues, soft lighting and hand lotion. It's an added incentive to women who loathe using public restrooms. Pamper the ladies with items specifically designed to turn a restroom into a powder room. Provide a baby changing station in both the ladies' and men's rooms.

- **Promote the spice of life.** Get things heated up by publicizing your free chips and salsa, or small vegetable crudités with dip to start. The offer will come in handy on busy nights when servers are swamped and need a few extra minutes of service time.

- **Promote your over-sized portions.** Have you ever been to a steak house that offers the meal free if the customer can eat it in one hour? You can do the same, or simply publicize the fact that your plates are stacked full and brimming with an abundance of tasty morsels.

- **Start a food fight.** Well, a one-way food fight, anyway. If your restaurant is one with a fun, young crowd of patrons, consider throwing rolls at your customers. One server walks around the dining room and tosses delicious rolls to customers who raise a flag on their table.

- **Give away calendars with coupons.** Insurance agents always have a minicalendar printed up to give to their customers. Why not do the same? Purchased in bulk, they're very inexpensive! Make sure each month has a handy coupon at the bottom for a discount on a meal.

- **Do what hotels do.** Offer a complimentary newspaper to your breakfast and early lunch customers.

- **Have a house phone.** Put up a sign that points to the area where free local calls can be made. It's a small amenity, but a service that guests will appreciate.

Rake In Report-Card Revenues

Education has been a top priority with many United States presidents. It's a also major concern for local educators who worry about the drop-out rate and the fact that many graduates are leaving high school without basic educational needs. You can help curb the catastrophe by promoting the fact that you believe in the young people in your community, and what's more, you're going to show your appreciation to those who strive to be the best they can be. Try the following ploys:

- **Discounts by the letter.** Parents are just as proud as the kids are about good grades. Offer discounts such as $1 off for every A and $0.50 off for every B.

- **Print some paraphernalia.** Use your logo and a catchy phrase combined to give away to straight-A students. Consider handing out things like T-shirts, pens, pencils and more!

- **Discount "bubbly."** How about offering discounts on bottles of sparkling cider to accompany the celebration dinners?

Boomerang Incentives

The boomerang effect is when a customer leaves and you work on getting him or her to turn around and come right back through the door again - within a certain period of time. There are many ways you can do this. The following are three of the top incentives that you can implement in order to get customers returning again and again and boosting your sales through the roof:

- **Drum up discounts.** Have a bowl at the lobby entrance where customers can deposit their business cards to win a dinner for two. Take those business cards and use them to send out mailers on your business promotions. You could also use early-bird specials or "come back" coupons.

- **Special-event promotions.** Make sure that your customers know what you offer when it's their birthday or anniversary. Treat them to a special meal. Get their information into a computerized database! Offer a small version of a cake or a free meal. Denny's is best known for its free birthday meals, for instance. You could also give certain things away for holidays or special events, such as Christmas cookies, or roses for Valentine's Day.

- **Promote a customer loyalty program.** You sometimes need to give customers a reason other than good service to come back, especially if other establishments are doing it, too. Punch cards are an option, but sometimes it's good just to have the manager come up to the table and tell regulars, "Desserts are on the house." It will make them feel like a million bucks.

Activity Stub Sensations

Giving back to the community doesn't stop with volunteer efforts. It's equally important to keep the economy running in order to ensure growth and increased revenues for your neighboring business counterparts. If you advertise on a regular basis, you might consider changing your Friday slot to an activity promotion, where you feature the local entertainment events and encourage people to attend them before they come in to dine. Try the following:

- **Show your movie or theater stub.** You can give a discount either to attendees of a particular movie cinema or theater or to those who saw a certain performance. Have them bring in their stub and give them a 10 percent discount.

- **Bring in your ballpark stub.** Many cities thrive when sports teams who are successful move into the area. Also, teams thrive when attendance is high. Offer an incentive to your customers who attend the local games and show their fandom to the stars.

Give Them a Vacation of a Lifetime

Some of the most-fantasized-about vacation destinations are the beautiful islands of Hawaii. Maui, Oahu and Hawaii tantalize visitors from all over the world to come experience the splendor of sun, surf and satisfaction that the islands have to offer. When visitors go to the islands, they almost always sign up for the local entertainment possibilities, which include special food presentations, parties and dancing till daylight. You can recreate this destination for your patrons who have been there and miss it and, of course, for those who may not ever have the chance to go. Here's how:

- **Have a luau.** Make it a Hawaiian shirt night for your servers, and encourage the customers to come in dressed that way, too. Shorts and straw hats will complete the ensemble.

- **Serve Hawaiian fare.** Think sweet and sour. Pineapples, pork, you name it. You might want to recreate the food served at a luau as well.

- **Tickets for two to Hawaii.** Travel companies would love to sponsor a free trip, as long as their name gets much of the attention in the press. How do you think radio stations get to give away so many trips and tickets? Promos say it all! Don't be afraid to just ask. Learn everything you need to know at www.hawaii.com.

Many People Love March Madness

March is the season for college basketball to come into the spotlight and take control of many sports enthusiasts around the country. While football may be the prime indicator of sports fanaticism in your locale, don't forget about college basketball fans! Below are two ways you can have fun feeding the basketball fan while not spending much on the promotion itself:

- **Five-for-five deal.** When the fans come out, they come in full force - with friends. And most of the time, men can eat a lot while watching their favorite team, so why not serve up five sandwiches, appetizers, or bottles of beer in buckets for $5?

- **Have a candy-tosser.** You don't have to use candy, but make sure that whenever the favorite team scores, something is tossed into the hands of your patrons. You also can use party favors to make noise for each score to boost the liveliness of the crowd.

Eye and Ear Catchers

Sometimes, you have to be seen and heard to get the word out about your local cuisine! The following are seven lucky ways guaranteed to attract the attention of the locals and increase your incoming traffic at the same time:

- **Movie theater pre-promotions.** These days, movie theaters have approximately 15-20 minutes' worth of commercials before the actual movie starts. Advertise the delights of your establishment on the big screen. You'll have a captive audience!

- **Skywriting.** Any time there's an outdoor festivity, hire a skywriter to streak the skies above the crowd with your business name. Look up and order now at www.skysigns.com.

- **Air banners.** If you've ever watched the show Big Brother, you know the fascination with air banners. Even the antismoking truth campaign used it in one of their ads to show how people at the beach were all enthralled with the flying banner.

- **Grocery-store shopping carts.** It's something we all have to do - grocery shopping. What better place to promote your business than when the customer is shopping for food and is probably hungry, too! Grocery-store carts now serve as mini billboards, so put an ad on them and watch sales soar.

- **Radio jingle.** Ever heard a silly tune on the radio while driving along that you couldn't seem to shake later on? Radio jingles can be a fun way to get the public singing your praises all day long - whether they want to or not !

- **Neon signs.** There's no better way to catch the eye of a passerby at night than with a smooth-looking neon sign that publicizes a special you're having. Not your company name, mind you, but a Happy Hour sign, or a Ladies' Night light-up. Order yours at www.abissigns.com.

- **Window cling-on.** Window cling-ons are the same kind you see at Christmas time, with cute Rudolph the Red-Nosed Reindeers and Frosty the Snow Mans on them. Get bigger ones that serve as shades as well to hand out to customers. Ask your staff to use them too.

CHAPTER SIX

POINT-OF-SALE PROMOTIONS

Catching Customers' Attention

There are numerous ways to advertise and get publicity all around town. But many people forget to promote their business on-site as a way to gain respect and marketability with their new customers. You have to treat all customers as if they're either first-timers and you're trying to impress them, or old-timers, whose patronage you know you couldn't bear losing. Making them feel special is a key concern. Never count on the fact that they'll be returning. Instead, set up in-store or point-of-sale promotions to let them know you're trying your hardest to get them back in the door at a later date. Here are a few suggestions for catching the customers' attention:

- **Discount coupons.** Tried and tested, a discount is a major incentive for consumers to choose one establishment over another. So in order to boost sales, you need to indulge them a little. It will pay dividends in the long run.

- **Contests.** Contests and giveaways are big items in the restaurant biz. Here are a couple of ways you can hold contests without breaking the bank, or having to go to another retailer to ask for a donation:

- **Counting games.** Have a jar of jellybeans, or a number of other items. Ask guests to fill out a guessing card in order to win the prize. Make sure it's stacked full of items, so it will be more difficult for them to figure out.

- **Children's coloring contest.** Once you have your logo designed, hold a contest for kids to color the black-and-white version of your logo for a chance to win a gift certificate to a major toy store. Then, plaster the walls with the colored-in logos for a short time. Tell parents that next time they come in, they can find their child's picture on the wall and take it home.

- **Scratch-off coupons.** Any local printer can prepare your very own personalized lottery ticket, but if you'd rather not pay for them to be personalized, you can purchase generic tickets that scratch off combination numbers. Three fives in a row could mean $5 off the total!

Random Promos to Keep Them on Their Toes

The unexpected is always a good way to get people to come back in the door. These are promos you don't want to publicize, but rather offer on a regular basis, so that people begin talking about them to their friends. Consider sending a press release to the editor of the local paper so he or she can spread the word too. However, refrain from advertising such a promo, unless you know ahead of time what your long-term plans are for using it. Bear in mind the following information:

- **Date-of-birth discount.** One night when you open, inform your servers that those customers who were born on a certain day, month or year are to get a discount or freebie at their meal. Be sure not to publicize it ahead of time. Ask for proof of identification, such as a driver's license, to verify eligibility.

- **"Put your license to good use" promotion.** Nobody likes his or her driver's license picture, but it can be put to good use: Have customers show you the first digit of their driver's license number. Give those with winning digits a discount or free drink on the house.

- **Clothing-brand blowout.** Depending on what's in style at the time, consider teaming up with a local retailer or clothing manufacturer. Give away one article of clothing (such as a T-shirt) to customers who happen to be wearing that same brand when they come to visit. Again, don't publicize it ahead of time – or they may take the shirt off your back!

- **Following the ABCs of promotions.** Randomly choose a letter of the alphabet. For customers whose name begins with that letter, offer 10 percent off.

Pleasantries That Will Shock and Delight Them

Just like the unexpected contests, promotions that aren't planned can have an intoxicating effect on your clientele. Below is a list of five pleasant extras that you can implement to increase patronage instantly. Try the following:

- **Car wash while you eat.** Find a local school who wants to raise some money. Invite them to hold a car wash in your parking lot. While customers dine, the kids wash their cars for FREE. Later on, you donate 10 percent of sales to the school – an awesome community contribution.

- **Rainy-day delights.** Rain can be pleasant for some, but blah for others. Why not offer one free drink or a free cookie to patrons on days when it's pouring outside?

- **Play golf.** Well, at least drive the cart! If your parking lot is large and packed on busy nights, have a golf cart on hand to pick up patrons and deliver them to the front door. Do the same for those who are leaving. Drop them off right at their car door.

- **Say "cheese!"** Have a Polaroid on hand to snap pictures of groups, couples, families and others that want to remember the night of fun and fare at your establishment. Better yet, use a digital camera and place them on your Web site. Order custom paper frames with your name printed on them for promotional value for years to come: check out www.qlt.com, www.outofthis-world.com and www.shiveximindia.com/photoframes.html.

- **Make a toast.** Whenever you find out a couple is celebrating their anniversary or a wedding party is in the house, get everyone's attention and make a special toast to the couple. Need a book on toasts? Check out www.atlantic-pub.com.

Celebrate the Restaurant's Anniversary

Don't forget to mark the day you first opened your doors. It goes a long way with the community. If your establishment has been in business for 25 years, say so with flair! If you've shared in the community for one year, celebrate that too! Here are four ways to promote your commitment to the locals and celebrate the fact that patrons have enjoyed your restaurant so much that your doors are still open:

- **Turn back the clock.** If you opened in 1980, then turn the prices back for one day to show your appreciation for your customers. If prices aren't that different, then have customers sign a guest book to tell what their favorite part of that year was.

- **Celebrate with gifts.** But in reverse! Give them gifts for their continued business, or offer party favors when they leave for the night, filled with silly items and coupons to get them back another day.

- **Host a party.** If you really want some coverage, close the doors for a night. Hold a big bash where only loyal, regular customers, local celebrities and the media are invited to attend.

- **Give away a classic car.** Did your family-owned place of business open in 1956? Buy a 1956 Pink Cadillac like the one Elvis bought for his mom and have it restored as a major prize giveaway. Think it might be too costly? Not if you find a mechanic willing to share in the promotion coverage you'll get from the local media. Patrons can come in and fill out an entry form that their waitperson gives them at the end of each meal. Find a classic to spruce up at www.caam.com.

Get 'Em Running

There are many reasons why races are held in communities nowadays. Sometimes they're held for a cause, such as breast cancer awareness or AIDS research. Other times, they're held just for fun. One of the main factors in each of these runs is who is going to sponsor the event. Who will be there to give out T-shirts, hand water to the runners and do other tasks? Maximize on the scenario. Get some publicity from the runners in your area by doing one or more of the following:

- **Create your own run.** Pick a cause. Or, simply do it for fun. Send out a press release telling the media when and where you plan to hold your run and, most importantly, why.

- **Sponsor an existing run.** There are many Web sites that list the various marathons and races all over the country. Find out which ones are coming to your area and then sign on to sponsor the runners!

- **Plan ahead.** Look in your Yellow Pages to find out if there are any local runners' groups that you can work with to help set up an event for them.

- **Make your restaurant the finish line.** You can have the race loop around so that it begins and ends right in your parking lot.

- **Sign on others.** Many other local businesses will love the chance to be cosponsors with you and participate in the running event. Sign on businesses that complement both your business and the runners in some way, such as a sporting goods store. That way, you have no competition, and the runners can get freebies they can use!

Silliness Can Be Satisfying

Sometimes it's fun to get the patrons involved in making fools out of themselves, as long as they're willing to play along! In order to make this kind of promotion work, you have to make sure it's an option for your customers - not something they have to do. Here are some suggestions:

- **Cluck like a chicken**. Burger King launched a special chicken sandwich. To get customers involved, they announced that you had to cluck like a chicken to get the $0.50 coupon! If you serve a chicken dish, you can do the same.

- **Moo like a cow.** Serving up a special steak dinner? A "Beef BBQ Buffet"? Customers who moo like a cow can get a dollar off their next meal coupon.

- **Oink like a pig.** Pork, sausage and ham eaters can oink like a pig to get their discount. Give away cute pig noses for the kids to wear. Find them at www.costumefun.com.

Transportation Touting Methods

Transportation methods are a great way to pack a punch in your publicity campaign. Just by using traveling vehicles, you're reaching more people than you would with a static promotion. Try one or more of these six methods and we guarantee you'll see an increase in in-house traffic:

- **Windshield-wiper coupons.** If there are several large parking lots in your area, consider hiring college students to place flyers with coupons on them under a windshield wiper of each car. Minimum wage usually pulls it off, and they can cover a large amount of space in an hour.

- **Park-and-ride fun fare.** Big time event or concert coming tonight? Have customers park in your lot and enjoy dinner first. Then, give everyone a ride to the big game on a special bus full of fans of the home team!

- **Turn your delivery van into a billboard.** Ever heard of the companies who pay people to wear wraps on their car? You can do the same! Car wraps can be customized. Pay people who drive around town a lot for use of their moving space and put your name on it. Order your materials at www.adsonwheels.com.

- **Balloon rides.** Hot-air balloons are a great way to attract customers all around town. Use a tethered balloon to lift customers up into the sky, and then bring them back to the ground - just in time to eat dinner at your establishment!

- **Put a twist on the car wash.** Make it a pet wash day! The media will love covering it, because pets tug at the heartstrings of everyone in the audience. You could even invite the Humane Society down to hold an adopt-a-pet marathon in your parking lot!

- **Transit vehicles.** Whether you promote your restaurant on the exterior of the transit vehicle or the interior, you're sure to have a ton of coverage in the end.

*Monthly promotions are
a good way to keep
customers coming back.*

CHAPTER SEVEN

MONTHLY MARKETING FOR PROMOTIONS & PUBLICITY

Make a Success of Monthly Marketing

On a month-to-month basis, you'll want to generate some new, exciting publicity for your restaurant. In order to achieve this goal, the following chapters offer a month-by-month guide to off-the-wall and traditional promotional ideas that you can easily implement in an instant. But first, here are a few general pointers to help you boost sales and keep customers returning every month:

- **The "unexpected."** The public generally expects restaurants and other retailers in the area to do some sort of promotion, even if it's as simple as a rose for every lady on Valentine's Day. However, the promotions that make people remember your name are the ones you do on days they don't expect anything!

- **Raise expectations about next month's "spectacular."** Introduce an air of mystery, excitement and anticipation. Customers will want to come back every month just to see what you have in store. You could even double your involvement in these promotions. Take steps to send off notices to the local media about every single one.

- **What if your monthly events don't achieve the desired coverage?** Then just place an ad in the local paper, preferably in their dining section if they have one, where newcomers and locals will think to check when they want a new place or new idea for eating out. Mail and e-mail your monthly newsletter.

January Jamborees

January is the time when everyone gets to start anew. They're thinking about all the various ways they can improve their lives. From health and fitness to marriage, family and career, every aspect is under strict scrutiny and in need of an injection of fresh ideas and better organization. Here are some odd (and not-so-odd), real-life holidays that could help you push your publicity campaign through the roof:

- **National Thank-You-Customer Week.** From January 7 to 11, you could publicize that, to show your appreciation for your customers, you'll be giving everyone a buy-one-get-one-free meal deal.

- **Fire the Boss Week.** From January 14 to 20, you could encourage those who are stalled in their career to fire their boss and find new employment opportunities. You could even hold a job fair in the parking lot for area businesses. Send out flyers to local colleges.

- **Healthy Weight Week.** January 21 to 27 is the time when you could hold a health fair to help your customers get fit. Ask a local not-for-profit organization to come by and offer free or low-cost evaluations.

- **Celebration of Life Month.** January is the time when we reevaluate our lives, so why not celebrate them in the process? Find out who the oldest local resident is. Invite him or her in for a celebration.

- **National Book Month.** Oprah has a book club, why can't you? You could invite local guest authors to come in for a reading. Or, let them set up shop in the lobby to sign copies of their works. Produce your own cookbook!

- **National Soup Month.** Serve it up! Have a day or two each week devoted to an array of unusual soups that your customers may not have had the chance to try. Find out their opinions on which ones they want kept on the menu and which ones are better left unprepared.

- **Fat-Free Living Month.** For the whole month of January, offer at least one fat-free item on your menu. Target specifically those who are jump-starting their diets this month.

- **National Lose Weight/Feel Great Month.** Instead of fat-free fare, try to offer a whole new take on low-calorie meals that will tantalize your customers' taste buds and tempt them back for more. Be sure to send out notices to local Weight Watchers groups too!

February Favorites

February has long been associated with love because of the overwhelming influence of the Valentine's holiday. But truth be told, this month is full of great opportunities for you to boost sales and build a spot for yourself in the community. Follow some of these tips to promote and publicize the success of your place of business, and you'll find your bank account growing and your building overflowing:

- **Cater to the cultural revolution.** February is Black History Month. Many museums and other cultural centers bring about awareness of this celebration, but few restaurants, if any, do. Be the first on your block to boost the pride of the black population in their heritage.

- **Sign on for the Special Olympics.** February is the time of the Special Olympics Winter Games. Why not hold a local Special Olympics in your own town for the local participants? Give customers an incentive to eat at your place: $0.15 on the dollar benefits the Special Olympics fund.

- **International Friendship Month.** Host a local celebration that encompasses all of the citizens in your city who make up the great melting pot of America. People love to promote the fact that they come from Irish, African or Hispanic backgrounds. A festival with fare from all around the world would go over great!

- **Celebration of Love Week.** The traditional February 14th holiday just isn't enough! Invite loving couples to join you in a week-long celebration from the 10th to the 16th.

- **Second Honeymoon Week.** When romance dies, you can help revive it by inviting couples, during the week of the 25th, to renew their love and maybe win a second honeymoon package!

- **Groundhog Day.** Did the little guy see his shadow on the 2nd or not? Be ready to launch an end-of-winter or not-yet-spring celebration when the weatherman announces the superstitious fate of our weather.

- **Pay a Compliment Day.** Instruct your staff that on the 6th, every single customer is to receive a compliment. Customers won't even know it's a holiday, and they'll leave with a boost of self-confidence.

- **Presidents' Day.** With a renewed sense of patriotism, you can honor the president on his special day, February 19. Have a contest where the best presidential look-alike wins a prize!

March Meal Deals

March is the month when people begin renewing their commitment to their January resolutions. They started out great, began slipping that month, and by February, it had all gone out the window. Help your customers get back on track with a slew of satisfying solutions that will help them create a better atmosphere and celebrate their on-track lifestyles with a meal at your restaurant. Consider the following opportunities:

- **Biking Week.** Hold a race around town for the bikers in your area the first week of March. The entry fees can even go to benefit a cause, such as breast cancer or a pediatric foundation.

- **Girl Scout Week.** The first week of March is also a tribute to the long-standing foundation known as the Girl Scouts. To help the cause, why not allow the troops to set up shop outside the front door to sell their famous cookies to your customers?

- **International Women's Day.** Women worldwide are celebrating their growing independence and added responsibilities. Celebrate this holiday on the 8th by hosting a Workingwoman's Wednesday.

- **Employee Appreciation Day.** The 7th is also another kind of celebration. Send out announcements to all of the local businesses telling them that you're offering a special deal for bosses to buy gift certificates for their employees or for group parties hosted by the company.

- **Incredible Kid Day.** Kids deserve to be celebrated, too! Hold a contest and announce it to the press for parents who want to win a family night out - dinner included. The winner will be announced on the 15th. Whichever parent writes the most compelling 250-word essay about why his or her children are so incredible wins.

- **Spring Fever Week.** Everyone has it at this time of year: an intense desire for summer to come along, and spring is just the beginning. Celebrate it the week of the 19th by hosting a Spring Fling where couples can dance, and customers can eat a light and fun-fare buffet.

- **National Family Day.** Families are a different animal than they were 50 years ago. Rarely do they sit down together for a meal. On the 24th, invite local families to your restaurant to participate in a true, old-fashioned family get-together.

- **Cleaning Week.** The week of the 25th is officially Spring Cleaning Week. Mothers will be busy dusting out the house, while dads will be trying to get their garages in order. Hold a giveaway for a free maid service or a professional organizer to come in one day.

April Acclaim

April is an awesome time to promote your business to customers who don't have anything else to celebrate that month. They're looking for a reason to get out and come to eat specifically at your restaurant. Give it to them! Try the following:

- **Alcohol Awareness Month.** This is the perfect time for you to promote responsible drinking. Offer a freebie to the designated drivers who join a group of drinkers. It can be a free meal or free sodas. Promote a complete menu of nonalcoholic drinks.

- **Customer Loyalty Month.** They are patrons of your place of business all year. Now give something back to them! Give your customer a Frequent Diner's Card with some added incentives this month.

- **National Lawn and Garden Month.** It may not have anything to do with restaurants, but it's a special way you can launch a promotion the guys will love too! Either find a lawn equipment manufacturer that will donate a prize for the handymen who patron your restaurant, or give away a lawn prize package!

- **National Zoo Month.** Your local zoo is always holding various promotions to increase their sponsorship. If you ask, they'll almost always provide you with free discount coupons you can give away to your customers.

- **National Reading Is Fun Month.** The First Lady has launched an initiative to increase readership in America. Host a reading program where you have a contest for the most books read or best essay about a particular book. What do you give as a prize? A gift certificate to a bookstore, of course!

- **Karaoke Month.** If your ears can handle it, rent a karaoke machine and a DJ to oversee it. Customers will have a blast showing off their talents – or lack thereof. Or, buy your own machine at www.karaokecenter.com.

- **National Sibling Day.** The 10th is a day to celebrate brothers and sisters. Offer a buy-one-get-one-free promotion to siblings who come to dine on this day.

- **Arbor and Earth Day.** The 22nd is both Arbor Day and Earth Day. Publicize your involvement in the community by planting trees. Clean up a local area that needs improvement.

May Merriment

May is the month where mothers are hailed as matriarch of the family, and springtime celebrations are on the rise as the weather permits them – with sun-filled days and long, light-soaked evenings. Take care of your customers by implementing some of these cozy concepts that will promote a union within the neighborhood:

- **BBQ Month.** Finger-lickin' good sauces and smoked ribs always go over well with any crowd. Hold an outdoor barbeque that lets people mingle while they eat. Be sure to have plenty of napkins on hand!

- **Senior Citizens' Month.** May is a great time to contact local senior groups and living residences to offer a promotion that celebrates our elderly citizens! Give them a special senior discount that isn't normally on the menu.

- **Family Week.** The week of the 6th is a special time when families are supposed to try to bond and form a stronger link to one another. Offer an incentive - like letting kids eat free - for mom and dad to bring the kids in and sit down together for a fun-filled meal.

- **Salvation Army Week.** The second week of May is a tribute to the Salvation Army, which cares for the poor in our community and helps families and individuals alike. Set up a special place in-house where patrons can donate canned goods and clothing to the Salvation

Army.

- **Police Week.** The week of the 13th is a celebration of those who protect and serve. Send an announcement that you want to not only honor those men and women, but also their families, who live with the possibility of their loved one encountering violence on a daily basis.

- **Friends Week.** The sitcom *Friends* has been a blockbuster hit since it came on the scene many years ago. Why not hold a *Friends* celebration of your own during the week of the 20th? Try a friends-eat-free promo, which can be essentially a buy-one-get-one-free deal.

- **No Diet Day.** Throw out the calorie counters on the 6th! Today is the day to treat your customers to splurges beyond their wildest imagination. Have an indulgence day, where every food served is a rich, intoxicating delight to the taste buds.

- **Teacher Day.** Teachers are one of the primary forces shaping the future of our world. Honor these treasures by giving them a day on the 7th where they receive a major discount or freebie for their service to the community.

- **Eat What You Want Day.** Similar to the No Diet Day, the Eat What You Want Day is a day when anything goes. To put a unique twist on it, try serving fare that isn't common in your area.

June Jubilation

June is a time for weddings and celebrations in the great outdoors. It's the end of spring and the introduction of summertime festivities, which send soothing invitations to citizens in the community that it's time to get out and mingle. Incorporate some of these promotions to remind patrons that summertime fun is just around the corner – and that you're ready to start early! Consider the following ideas for June:

- **Kids' Month.** June is officially Kids' Month, so why not make it kids' month in your business as well? Once a week, invite a local artistic person to entertain the little ones with fun, such as mimes, painting, pottery, clowns, storytellers and more!

- **Taco Day.** The 12th is a day dedicated to the devotion of tacos. No kidding! So even if your restaurant isn't a Mexican genre, you can whip up some taco wraps made with some of your own personal fare.

- **Splurge Day.** June 19th is National Splurge Day, so you can either splurge on your customers with a free sinful dessert or have a splurge promo where you encourage them to splurge for a day.

- **Baby Boomers Recognition Day.** Yes, they have their own day on the 21st! Cater to the Baby Boomer generation by serving up items that were a favorite in the era when they were teens and just beginning to venture out for dining experiences without their parents.

- **America's Kids Day.** We hear a lot of news stories about efforts being made to improve the lives of foreign children. Bring the message home to the hearts of the community and plan a party for a local orphanage or women and children's shelter to show the kids you care.

July Joy

Summertime is here! The sizzling summer joys are upon us, and patrons are ready to dress up and go out for a night on the town! It's also a time for family picnics and outdoor fun. Luckily, the summer months mean more hours of sunlight each evening, so you can plan on staying open later throughout the season if you want to – and rake in the business that goes along with it!

- **Have a community picnic.** In the old days, neighbors would hold block parties where each participant would bring a favorite dish to share. You can do the same. Either host a parking lot party, where you cater all of the fare, or invite a bakery to provide the desserts and other companies to join in setting up an outdoor buffet. Be sure to include entertainment. Some bands will do it for free for the coverage and exposure it provides!

- **Cow Appreciation Day.** Ever seen the billboards where the cows are painting "Eat more chicken" signs to promote Chick-Fil-A? Well, have a "Be Kind to Cows" day on the 13th where you remove all beef from the menu and replace it with chicken delights!

August Activities

August can be a very exciting time. Summer is ending, and parents want to entertain their children, who are reluctantly about to go back to school. Having some fun with these publicity stunts can help ease the transition from summertime fun to serious studies. Try the following suggestions:

- **Family Fun Month.** It's officially Family Fun Month, so help the families out by giving away discount coupons for theme parks in your area. With seasonal closings right around the corner, they'll want to drum up enough business to boost their bank accounts through the winter. You can even give away a pair of free tickets to one lucky couple!

- **Back to School Month.** Although some schools start back in September, most call the kids back in August. Contact your local superstores to see if they'd be willing to donate a back-to-school package with a new backpack and lunch box and school supplies. If you're resourceful, a nice letter to the manufacturer of Lunchables meals might produce some freebies for you to give away as well!

- **Elvis Week.** The 10th through the 16th is National Elvis Week. Call in an impersonator to walk around and entertain the crowds on the weekend. Send out a press release so that the paper runs a story about a contest that you're holding for the best Elvis look-alike. The winner gets a free dinner – a fried peanut butter and banana sandwich, maybe?

- **Sisters' Day.** There's a strong bond between siblings, especially sisters, who have borrowed each other's clothes over the years and shared their tears over boyfriends who have wronged them. Publicize your special Sisters' Day where siblings get a discount on their total bill.

- **Golf Month.** At any store like K-Mart or Wal-Mart, you can pick up a very inexpensive indoor putting green. Have a couple of putters on hand and invite customers to try for a hole-in-one. Those who get it also get a truffle in the shape of a golf ball for dessert (found at any grocery store in the candy aisle). One shot only per customer!

September Shenanigans

September is officially Back-to-Business Month. The kids are in school, and everything is back on schedule. Here are six new ways you can deliver a celebratory style for the month of September:

- **National Student Day.** The 20th is a special day when students are honored for their achievements and efforts. Launch a "straight A" campaign this month, where straight-A students are given a report card coupon for you to punch every time they bring in perfect grades that year.

- **Singles week.** From the 16th to the 22nd, you can bring singles together for a match-making extravaganza! Invite a local service to host a party at your restaurant where patrons can mix and mingle while enjoying a buffet-style dinner.

- **Pregnant Women's Day.** Expectant mothers love to be pampered! The 8th is a special day when mommies-to-be can come to your place of business for a special luncheon and presentation by someone in the community. You can even bring in a representative from Creative Memories to help prepare them for preserving the precious memories of their children - before the big day even arrives!

- **Grandparents' Day.** Schools in your area might allow children to bring in grandma or grandpa for a lunch together on the 9th, but you can go one step further. Invite the whole family in to honor the grandparents that night for dinner!

- **National Food Service Employees Day.** Turn the tables on the celebrations and show some respect and appreciation to your own employees on the 26th. Publicize the special day for your customers to see and get them involved in voting for the employee of the day.

- **Eat Better Together Month.** Moms and dads have been searching for a way to get the kids to eat their veggies for ages! But this month, you can help them out by inventing fun new ways to serve up the greens and coax the kids into enjoying them!

October Occasions

October has traditionally been known as a month for Halloween shenanigans. However, many people don't celebrate the holiday and might appreciate a few more reasons to celebrate during the month of fall fun. Try a few of these promos to create a festive atmosphere for adults and kids alike, during the cool month of October. How about the following:

- **Boss' Day.** Most people are aware of Administrative Assistants' Day, but good bosses deserve to be honored too! Send out promotional invitations to local businesses where the secretary will probably be reading the incoming mail anyway. Get them to come in on the 16th for a deal where the boss eats free when his or her employees pay full price.

- **National Chili Week.** You can be the host of your own local chili contest, where the winner receives a cash prize, on the week of the 7th. Have plenty of beer and crackers on hand, and set up the contest outdoors, where patrons can walk around and sample the fare while they are entertained by music and fun.

- **Gumbo Day.** On the 12th, bring New Orleans Cajun fare to your doorstep! Serve up a special mix of gumbo delights that will tantalize the taste buds and spice up the atmosphere. If you really want to go all out, get a jazz band to play for the night as an added touch.

November Notoriety

November proves to be a very hectic month. Shoppers abound, with Thanksgiving, Christmas and football on their minds. What do they do while shopping for the holidays? Eat! Here are a few ways to make them swerve into your parking lot above all others:

- **Chicken Soup for the Soul Day.** During the holidays, nostalgia is on the minds of everyone. Hold a contest for the best "soul" essay and serve up a tummy-warming chicken soup for a day when the prize is given away. You can give away a winning T-shirt or gift certificate to the restaurant.

- **Veterans' Day.** Patriotism is at an all-time high. Veterans' Day has special meaning on the 11th, and you can show your stars and stripes by doing a "Veterans Eat Free" promotion. All they need is a military ID!

- **"Dear Santa" Letter-Writing Week.** Buy some pre-stamped postcards and hand them out, along with a crayon, to each child who comes in the week of the 5th, so that he or she can write a letter to Santa Claus. You can even have a staff member address it to the North Pole and set up a Santa Box at the exit so that children can deposit their outgoing letters at the end of the night.

December Diversions

With all of the in-your-face promos going on to attract shoppers' attention for holiday sales, it's tough to compete with all of the hubbub! Here are a couple of ways you can distance yourself from traditional December promos. Bring in people for a new reason. Try this approach:

- **Pearl Harbor Remembrance Day.** December 7 is a special day in all of our hearts. Even more so since September 11, 2001. Hold a Remembrance Day for those who served our country and those who serve today. Anyone wearing red, white and blue gets a discount on their meal.

- **Humbug Day.** Not everyone relishes the thought of Christmas! We live among people who prefer to show the Scrooge side of themselves every once in awhile. Have fun with it! On the 21st, invite everyone to be a grouch for a day! Give them all a break from the hectic crowds and cheer that overwhelms many of us during the holiday season.

There's a reason for promotion every day of the calendar year!

CHAPTER EIGHT

365 DAYS OF PROMOTIONS

Want More?

There's a reason for promotion every day of the year! Consider celebrating celebrity birthdays by having a look-alike contest with a free dinner for the winner. Or, offer 10 percent off any meal for customers who happen to have a picture of their pet on National Pet Day (January 14). This chapter has a calendar with events covering all 365 days of the year. The possibilities are endless! Consider the following:

- **Look for days to honor your loyal customers.** For example, if you serve a large population of senior citizens, consider a promotion for National Senior Citizens' Day (November 1). Your loyal customers will feel appreciated and may increase their patronage.

- **Introduce new menu items.** A special promotion can be a great time to experiment with new menu items. Try implementing new desserts on National Spumoni Day (August 21) to gauge popularity.

- **Don't overlook local opportunities.** Most cities have a local historic person, hero, festival or high school sporting event. These can be great opportunities to run a promotion that draws customers and promotes civic pride

January

1	2	3	4	5	6	7
Birthdays: Betsy Ross Paul Revere	National Science Fiction Day National Cream Puff Day	Drinking Straw Day Birthday: Mel Gibson	National Spaghetti Day First Road Sign	National Whipped Cream Day	National Shortbread Day Apple Tree Day	Typewriter Patented Birthdays: Nicolas Cage Katie Couric
8 National Clean-Off-Your-Desk Day Birthday: Elvis Presley	**9** National Apricot Day Birthday: Richard Nixon	**10** Volunteer Firemen's Day Barbed Wire Patent	**11** International Thank You Day Birthday: Alexander Hamilton	**12** National Marzipan Day First X-Ray Taken	**13** Frisbee Invented Accordion Patented	**14** Dress Up Your Pet Day Hot Pastrami Sandwich Day
15 National Strawberry Ice Cream Day Birthday: Martin Luther King Jr.	**16** National Fig Newton Day	**17** Pig Day Birthdays: Jim Carrey Muhammad Ali	**18** Jazz Day Birthday: Kevin Costner	**19** National Popcorn Day Birthday: Dolly Parton	**20** Cheese Day Basketball Day	**21** Hugging Day Birthday: Geena Davis
22 National Blonde Brownie Day	**23** Hand-writing Day National Pie Day	**24** National Peanut Butter Day	**25** Opposite Day First Winter Olympics Began	**26** National Peanut Brittle Day Birthday: Paul Newman	**27** National Chocolate Cake Day Birthday: Wolfgang A. Mozart	**28** National Blueberry Pancake Day
29 National Corn Chip Day Birthday: Oprah Winfrey	**30** National Croissant Day	**31** Child Labor Day				

National Health Month • National Oatmeal Month
National Soup Month

February

1 National Baked Alaska Day	**2** Groundhog Day	**3** National Carrot Day	**4** National Stuffed Mushroom Day	**5** National Weatherperson's Day	**6** National Frozen Yogurt Day	**7** National Fettuccine Alfredo Day
Birthday: Clark Gable	Birthday: Farrah Fawcett	Wedding Ring Day	Birthday: Charles Lindbergh		Birthday: Babe Ruth	Birthday: Laura Ingalls Wilder
8 Boy Scouts Day	**9** National Bagels & Lox Day	**10** School Day	**11** Don't Cry over Spilled Milk Day	**12** National Plum Pudding Day	**13** National Tortini Day	**14** National Heart to Heart Day
Kite Flying Day	Birthday: Carmen Miranda	Birthday: Greg Norman			Penicillin First Used on Humans	
15 National Gum Drop Day	**16** Do a Grouch a Favor Day	**17** Champion Crab Races Day	**18** National Battery Day	**19** National Chocolate Mint Day	**20** National Cherry Pie Day	**21** National Sticky Bun Day
Birthday: Susan B. Anthony	Birthday: Sonny Bono	Birthday: Michael Jordan	Birthday: John Travolta		Birthday: Cindy Crawford	Birthday: Kelsey Grammer
22 Be Humble Day	**23** International Dog Biscuit Appreciation Day	**24** National Tortilla Chip Day	**25** Hen Laid the Largest Egg	**26** National Pistachio Day	**27** International Polar Bear Day	**28** Red Spots of Jupiter
Birthday: Drew Barrymore		Birthday: Enrico Caruso	Birthday: George Harrison	Birthday: Levi Strauss	Birthday: Elizabeth Taylor	Birthday: Mario Andretti
29 National Surf & Turf Day						

National Dental Health Month
American Heart Month • Black History Month

March

1	2	3	4	5	6	7
Peanut Butter Lover's Day Birthday: Ron Howard	Old Stuff Day Birthday: Dr. Seuss	I Want You to Be Happy Day	National Poundcake Day Birthday: Knute Rockne	Stop the Clocks Day Birthday: Andy Gibb	National Frozen Food Day Birthday: Shaquille O'Neal	National Crown Roast of Pork Day
8	**9**	**10**	**11**	**12**	**13**	**14**
National Peanut Cluster Day Birthday: Micky Dolenz	National Crabmeat Day Panic Day	First Paper Money Issued Birthday: Sharon Stone	Worship of Tools Day Birthday: Lawrence Welk	Baked Scallops Day Birthday: Liza Minnelli	Uranus Discovered, 1781	National Potato Chip Day Birthdays: Billy Crystal Albert Einstein
15	**16**	**17**	**18**	**19**	**20**	**21**
Everything You Think Is Wrong Day	Everything You Do Is Right Day	St. Patrick's Day Birthday: Nat "King" Cole	Supreme Sacrifice Day	Poultry Day Birthdays: Bruce Willis Wyatt Earp	Festival of Extra-terrestrial Abductions Day	Fragrance Day National French Bread Day
22	**23**	**24**	**25**	**26** Make Up Your Own Holiday Day	**27**	**28**
National Goof-off Day Birthday: William Shatner	Organize Your Home Office Day National Chip & Dip Day	National Chocolate-Covered Raisins Day	Pecan Day Waffle Day Birthday: Howard Cosell	Spinach Festival Day	National Spanish Paella Day First Fire Engine Tested	Something on a Stick Day
29	**30**	**31**				
Coca-Cola Invented National Lemon Chiffon Cake Day	I Am in Control Day	Oranges & Lemons Day Tater Day				

American Red Cross Month · National Craft Month
National Peanut Butter Month

April

1	2	3	4	5	6	7
National Sourdough Bread Day One Cent Day	National Peanut Butter & Jelly Day	Don't Go to Work Unless It's Fun Day Birthday: Eddie Murphy	National Cordon Bleu Day Birthday: Maya Angelou	National Raisin & Spice Bar Day Birthday: Bette Davis	National Caramel Popcorn Day Modern Olympics Began	No Housework Day Birthday: Russell Crowe
8	9	10	11	12	13	14
National Empanada Day International Bird Day	Chinese Almond Cookie Day First Public Library Opened	Golfers Day Birthday: Haley Joel Osment	National Cheese Fondue Day Dandelion Day	Look Up at the Sky Day Birthday: David Letterman	Blame Somebody Else Day	National Pecan Day Birthday: Sarah Michelle Gellar
15	16	17	18	19	20	21
National Glazed Ham Day Birthday: Leonardo da Vinci	Stress Awareness Day National Eggs Benedict Day	National Cheeseball Day	Juggler's Day National Animal Crackers Day	Garlic Day Birthdays: Kate Hudson Ashley Judd	Look-Alike Day Pineapple Upside-Down Cake Day	Kindergarten Day Birthday: Elizabeth II, Queen of England
22	23	24	25	26	27	28
National Jelly Bean Day Birthday: Jack Nicholson	Read To Me Day World Laboratory Animal Day	Pigs in a Blanket Day Birthday: Barbra Streisand	National Zucchini Bread Day Birthday: Al Pacino	National Pretzel Day Richter Scale Day	National Prime Rib Day Write an Old Friend Today Day	Great Poetry Reading Day Kiss-Your-Mate Day
29	30					
National Shrimp Scampi Day Birthday: Jerry Seinfeld	National Honesty Day Birthday: Willie Nelson					

National Garden Month
Keep America Beautiful Month

May

1	2	3	4	5	6	7
National Chocolate Parfait Day May Day	National Truffles Day Birthday: Dwayne "The Rock" Johnson	Raspberry Popover Day National Day of Prayer	National Candied Orange Peel Day Birthday: Lance Bass	National Hoagie Day Birthday: Tammy Wynette	Beverage Day Nurses' Day	National Roast Leg of Lamb Day
8 National Teacher Day Birthday: Melissa Gilbert	**9** Butter-scotch Brownie Day Birthdays: Billy Joel Candice Bergen	**10** National Shrimp Day Clean Up Your Room Day	**11** Eat What You Want Day Twilight Zone Day	**12** Limerick Day Birthdays: George Carlin Yogi Berra	**13** National Apple Pie Day Casey at the Bat Published	**14** National Dance like a Chicken Day
15 National Chocolate Chip Day Birthday: Emmitt Smith	**16** Love a Tree Day First Envelope Made	**17** National Cherry Cobbler Day	**18** Visit Your Relatives Day Birthday: Reggie Jackson	**19** National Devil's Food Cake Day Armed Forces Day	**20** Flower Day Birthdays: Cher Jimmy Stewart	**21** National Waitresses/ Waiters Day National Memo Day
22 Buy a Musical Instrument Day	**23** Penny Day Birthdays: Jewel Drew Carey	**24** National Escargot Day Birthday: Bob Dylan	**25** National Tap Dance Day Birthday: Mike Myers	**26** National Blueberry Cheesecake Day	**27** National Grape Popsicle Day Golden Gate Bridge Fiesta	**28** National Hamburger Day Whale Day
29 Escalator Patented Birthdays: John F. Kennedy Bob Hope	**30** Ice Cream Freezer Patented First Hovercraft Launched	**31** National Macaroon Day Birthday: Clint Eastwood				

National BBQ Month

June

1	2	3	4	5	6	7
Doughnut Day Birthday: Marilyn Monroe	National Rocky Road Day Birthday: Jerry Mathers	Repeat Day Birthday: Tony Curtis	National Frozen Yogurt Day Cheese Day	Festival of Popular Delusions Day	National Applesauce Cake Day Birthday: Sandra Bernhard	National Chocolate Ice Cream Day
8 National Jelly-Filled Doughnut Day Vacuum Cleaner Patented	**9** International Young Eagles Day Birthday: Michael J. Fox	**10** National Yo-Yo Day Birthday: Judy Garland	**11** National Hug Holiday Birthday: Vince Lombardi	**12** Machine Day Birthday: George Bush	**13** Kitchen Klutzes of America Day	**14** Pop Goes the Weasel Day Flag Day
15 Smile Power Day Birthdays: Courteney Cox Helen Hunt	**16** National Hollerin' Contest Day	**17** Eat Your Vegetables Day	**18** International Picnic Day Birthday: Paul McCartney	**19** World Sauntering Day	**20** Ice Cream Soda Day Birthday: Nicole Kidman	**21** Cuckoo Warning Day Birthday: Maureen Stapleton
22 National Chocolate Eclair Day Birthday: Meryl Streep	**23** National Pink Day Typewriter Invented	**24** Museum Comes to Life Day	**25** Log Cabin Day Birthdays: Jimmie Walker Carly Simon	**26** National Chocolate Pudding Day	**27** National Orange Blossom Day Birthday: Helen Keller	**28** Paul Bunyan Day
29 Camera Day Birthdays: Gary Busey Richard Lewis	**30** Meteor Day Birthday: Mike Tyson					

National Dairy Month • National Rose Month

July

1	2	3	4	5	6	7
Creative Ice Cream Flavor Day Canada Day	National Literacy Day Birthday: Richard Petty	Stay out of the Sun Day Compliment Your Mirror Day	National Country Music Day Birthday: Geraldo Rivera	Work-aholics Day Birthday: P.T. Barnum	National Fried Chicken Day	National Strawberry Sundae Day
8	**9**	**10**	**11**	**12**	**13**	**14**
Video Games Day Birthday: Kevin Bacon	National Sugar Cookie Day Birthday: Tom Hanks	Wyoming Admission Day Birthday: Jessica Simpson	National Cheer Up the Lonely Day	National Pecan Pie Day Birthday: Bill Cosby	Fool's Paradise Day Birthday: Harrison Ford	National Nude Day
15	**16**	**17**	**18**	**19**	**20**	**21**
National Tapioca Pudding Day	Celebrate Air-Conditioning Day	National Peach Ice Cream Day	National Caviar Day Birthday: John Glenn	Thank Your Mother Day Birthday: Anthony Edwards	Thank Your Father Day	National Catfish Day Birthdays: Robin Williams Don Knotts
22	**23**	**24**	**25**	**26**	**27**	**28**
Canine Appreciation Day Birthday: Alex Trebek	National Vanilla Ice Cream Day	Amelia Earhart Day Birthday: Jennifer Lopez	Threading the Needle Day	All or Nothing Day Birthdays: Sandra Bullock Kevin Spacey	Take Your Pants for a Walk Day	National Milk Chocolate Day
29	**30**	**31**				
Cheese Sacrifice Purchase Day	Cheesecake Day Birthday: Arnold Schwarz-enegger	Parents' Day Birthday: Wesley Snipes				

National Ice Cream Month

August

1	2	3	4	5	6	7
Friendship Day National Raspberry Cream Pie	National Ice Cream Soda Day Ice Cream Sandwich Day	National Watermelon Day Birthday: Martha Stewart	Twins Day Festival Birthdays: Jeff Gordon Billy Bob Thornton	National Mustard Day	Wiggle Your Toes Day Birthday: Lucille Ball	Sea Serpent Day Birthday: David Duchovny
8	**9**	**10**	**11**	**12**	**13**	**14**
Sneak Some Zucchini Onto Your Neighbor's Porch Night	National Polka Festival Birthday: Melanie Griffith	Lazy Day Birthday: Jimmy Dean	Presidential Joke Day Birthday: Hollywood Hulk Hogan	Middle Child's Day Birthday: Pete Sampras	Blame Someone Else Day	National Creamsicle Day
15	**16**	**17**	**18**	**19**	**20**	**21**
National Relaxation Day National Failures Day	Bratwurst Festival Birthdays: Madonna Kathie Lee Gifford	National Thriftshop Day Birthday: Robert De Niro	Bad Poetry Day Birthday: Robert Redford	Potato Day Birthdays: Bill Clinton Matthew Perry	National Radio Day Birthday: Connie Chung	National Spumoni Day Birthday: Kenny Rogers
22	**23**	**24**	**25**	**26**	**27**	**28**
Be an Angel Day Birthday: Valerie Harper	National Spongecake Day	Knife Day Birthday: Cal Ripken, Jr.	Kiss-and-Make-Up Day	National Cherry Popsicle Day	Petroleum Day Birthday: Mother Teresa	World Sauntering Day
29	**30**	**31**				
More Herbs, Less Salt Day Birthday: Michael Jackson	National Toasted Marsh-mallow Day	National Trail Mix Day Birthday: Richard Gere				

Family Fun Month

September

1	2	3	4	5	6	7
Emma M. Nutt Day Birthday: Lily Tomlin	National Beheading Day	Skyscraper Day Birthday: Charlie Sheen	Newspaper Carrier Day Birthday: Damon Wayans	Be Late for Something Day	Fight Procrast-ination Day Birthday: Jane Curtin	Neither Rain nor Snow Day
8	**9**	**10**	**11**	**12**	**13**	**14**
National Date Nut Bread Day Pardon Day	Teddy Bear Day Birthdays: Adam Sandler Hugh Grant	Swap Ideas Day Birthday: Arnold Palmer	No News Is Good News Day	National Chocolate Milkshake Day	Defy Superstition Day Birthday: Mel Torme	National Cream-Filled Donut Day
15	**16**	**17**	**18**	**19**	**20**	**21**
Felt Hat Day Birthday: Oliver Stone	Collect Rocks Day Birthday: David Copperfield	National Apple Dumpling Day	National Play-Doh Day Birthday: Greta Garbo	National Butter-scotch Pudding Day	National Punch Day Birthday: Sophia Loren	The Birth of the Ice Cream Cone World Gratitude Day
22	**23**	**24**	**25**	**26**	**27**	**28**
Hobbit Day Dear Diary Day	Checkers Day Dogs in Politics Day	Festival of Latest Novelties Birthday: F. Scott Fitzgerald	National Comic Book Day Birthday: Will Smith	Good Neighbor Day National Pancake Day	Crush a Can Day Birthday: Meat Loaf	Ask a Stupid Question Day
29	**30**					
Blackberries Day Birthday: Jerry Lee Lewis	National Mud Pack Day Birthday: Jenna Elfman					

October

1 World Vegetarian Day Magic Circles Day	**2** Name Your Car Day Birthday: Groucho Marx	**3** Virus Appreciation Day Birthday: Neve Campbell	**4** National Golf Day Birthday: Susan Sarandon	**5** National Storytelling Festival Birthday: Kate Winslet	**6** German-American Day Come and Take It Day	**7** National Frappe Day Birthday: John Cougar Mellencamp
8 American Tag Day Birthdays: Matt Damon Chevy Chase	**9** Eat More Cheese Day Birthday: John Lennon	**10** National Angel Food Cake Day	**11** It's My Party Day Birthday: Joan Cusack	**12** International Moment of Frustration Scream Day	**13** National Peanut Festival Birthday: Nancy Kerrigan	**14** National Dessert Day Be Bald and Free Day
15 White Cane Safety Day	**16** Dictionary Day Birthday: Suzanne Somers	**17** Gaudy Day Birthday: Rita Hayworth	**18** No Beard Day Birthday: Jean-Claude Van Damme	**19** Evaluate Your Life Day	**20** National Brandied Fruit Day Birthday: Mickey Mantle	**21** Babbling Day Birthday: Carrie Fisher
22 National Nut Day Birthday: Jeff Goldblum	**23** National Mole Day Birthday: Johnny Carson	**24** National Bologna Day	**25** Put Your Feet Up Day Birthday: Pablo Picasso	**26** Mule Day Birthday: Hillary Rodham Clinton	**27** Celebrate Cows Day Birthday: Emily Post	**28** Plush Animal Lover's Day National Chocolate Day
29 Hermit Day Birthday: Winona Ryder	**30** National Candy Corn Day Birthday: Henry Winkler	**31** National Magic Day Increase Your Psychic Powers Day				

November

1	2	3	4	5	6	7
National Senior Citizens Day	National Deviled Egg Day Birthday: Marie Antoinette	Sandwich Day Housewife's Day	Waiting for the Barbarians Day	Gunpowder Day Birthday: Vivien Leigh	Saxophone Day Marooned without a Compass Day	National Bittersweet Chocolate with Almonds Day
8	**9**	**10**	**11**	**12**	**13**	**14**
Dunce Day Birthday: Bonnie Raitt	National Sweet Tooth Day Birthday: Lou Ferrigno	Forget-Me-Not Day	Celebrate the Beauty of Nature Day	National Pizza With The Works Except Anchovies Day	National Pudding Day Birthday: Whoopi Goldberg	Operation Room Nurse Day Birthday: Prince Charles
15	**16**	**17**	**18**	**19**	**20**	**21**
National Clean Out Your Fridge Day	Button Day Birthdays: Oksana Baiul Lisa Bonet	Take a Hike Day Birthday: Danny DeVito	National Wear Brown Shoes Day	Eat a Banana Day Birthday: Meg Ryan	Absurdity Day Birthday: Bo Derek	World Hello Day False Confessions Day
22	**23**	**24**	**25**	**26**	**27**	**28**
Start Your Own Country Day	National Cashew Day Birthday: Billy the Kid	National Dine Out Day	National Parfait Day Birthday: Joe DiMaggio	Shopping Reminder Day Birthday: Tina Turner	Pins and Needles Day Birthday: Jimi Hendrix	National Chicken Soup Day Birthday: Jon Stewart
29	**30**					
Square Dance Day Birthday: Garry Shandling	Stay at Home Because You're Well Day					

December

1	2	3	4	5	6	7
National Pie Day Eat a Red Apple Day	National Fritters Day Birthday: Britney Spears	National Roof-over-Your-Head Day	Honk Your Horn day Birthday: Marisa Tomei	National Sacher Torte Day Birthday: Walt Disney	National Gazpacho Day Mitten Tree Day	National Cotton Candy Day Birthday: Aaron Carter
8	9	10	11	12	13	14
Take It in the Ear Day Birthday: Kim Basinger	National Pastry Day Birthday: Donny Osmond	Festival for the Souls of Dead Whales	National Noodle Ring Day	National Ding-a-Ling Day Birthday: Frank Sinatra	Ice Cream and Violins Day	National Bouil-labaisse Day
15	16	17	18	19	20	21
National Lemon Cupcake Day	National Chocolate Covered Anything Day	Underdog Day National Maple Syrup Day	National Roast Suckling Pig Day	Oatmeal Muffin Day Birthday: Alyssa Milano	Games Day	Look at the Bright Side Day National Flashlight Day
22	23	24	25	26	27	28
National French Fried Shrimp Day	Birthday: Susan Lucci	National Egg Nog Day Birthday: Ricky Martin	National Pumpkin Pie Day Birthday: Humphrey Bogart	National Whiners Day Birthday: Steve Allen	National Fruitcake Day Birthday: Marlene Dietrich	Card Playing Day National Chocolate Day
29	30	31				
Pepper Pot Day Birthday: Mary Tyler Moore	Festival of Enormous Changes at the Last Minute	National Bicarbonate of Soda Day				

INDEX

If you enjoyed this book, order the entire series!

1-800-541-1336 Call toll-free
24 hours a day, 7 days a week.
Or fax completed form to:
1-352-622-5836 Order online!
Just go to **www.atlantic-pub.com**
for fast, easy, secure ordering.

Qty	Order Code	Book Title	Price	Total
	Item # RMH-02	THE RESTAURANT MANAGER'S HANDBOOK	$79.95	
	Item # FS1-01	Restaurant Site Location	$19.95	
	Item # FS2-01	Buying & Selling A Restaurant Business	$19.95	
	Item # FS3-01	Restaurant Marketing & Advertising	$19.95	
	Item # FS4-01	Restaurant Promotion & Publicity	$19.95	
	Item # FS5-01	Controlling Operating Costs	$19.95	
	Item # FS6-01	Controlling Food Costs	$19.95	
	Item # FS7-01	Controlling Labor Costs	$19.95	
	Item # FS8-01	Controlling Liquor, Wine & Beverage Costs	$19.95	
	Item # FS9-01	Building Restaurant Profits	$19.95	
	Item # FS10-01	Waiter & Waitress Training	$19.95	
	Item # FS11-01	Bar & Beverage Operation	$19.95	
	Item # FS12-01	Successful Catering	$19.95	
	Item # FS13-01	Food Service Menus	$19.95	
	Item # FS14-01	Restaurant Design	$19.95	
	Item # FS15-01	Increasing Restaurant Sales	$19.95	
	Item # FSALL-01	**Entire 15-Book Series**	**$199.95**	

➤ *Best Deal!* SAVE 33%
All 15 books for $199.95

Subtotal	
Shipping & Handling	
Florida 6% Sales Tax	
TOTAL	

SHIP TO:

Name_____ Phone(_____) _____

Company Name_____

Mailing Address _____

City _____ State _____ Zip _____

FAX _____ E-mail _____

❑ My check or money order is enclosed   ❑ Please send my order COD   ❑ My authorized purchase order is attached

❑ Please charge my: ❑ Mastercard   ❑ VISA   ❑ American Express   ❑ Discover

Card # ❑❑❑❑–❑❑❑❑–❑❑❑❑–❑❑❑❑   Expires ❑❑❑❑

Please make checks payable to: **Atlantic Publishing Company** • 1210 SW 23rd Place • Ocala, FL 34474-7014
USPS Shipping/Handling: add $5.00 first item, and $2.50 each additional or $15.00 for the whole set.
Florida residents PLEASE add the appropriate sales tax for your county.